# HOW TO
# PASS
# YOUR
# DRIVING
# TEST

# HOW TO PASS YOUR DRIVING TEST

With over 700 questions & answers on The Highway Code

**John Thorpe**
**Wendy Goss**

TREASURE PRESS

First published in Great Britain in 1989 as two separate volumes

under the titles 'How to Pass Your Driving Test ' and ' The Highway Code '

This omnibus edition published in 1991 by

Treasure Press

Michelin House

81 Fulham Road

London SW3 6RB

ISBN  1 85051 680 4

Printed and bound in the United Kingdom by The Bath Press

# Contents

# Driving Techniques

# Introduction

There's a cloud on the horizon of every learner driver – the driving test. It could hardly loom larger or blacker were it the tail end of Hurricane Charlie, and it is usually true to say that when the official appointment card arrives to confirm a time and place, the encounter is anticipated with much the same feelings of joy as a date with the Spanish Inquisition.

So the very first lesson to learn is not to be afraid of the test. If you have been conscientiously trained by a good professional instructor – and that means an ADI (Approved Driving Instructor) who holds a Diploma in Driving Instruction – you will encounter nothing in the test that is unfamiliar to you, except the official examiner.

You may find his lack of communication disconcerting – you will be used to your instructor occupying that seat, giving you helpful advice and telling you how to correct mistakes. That's his job. But it isn't the examiner's job: he is simply a skilled observer whose duty it is to ensure not that you make no mistakes, but that any you do make are neither serious nor dangerous. By the end of the test he has to have satisfied himself that your standards of roadcraft and car control are good enough to permit you to drive without supervision – nothing more, nothing less.

If you have taken the sensible precaution of having professional driving instruction you are likelier, instead, to become the proud possessor of an altogether more welcome form – a pass certificate; and you won't really care what *that* says. It's a fact that learners who have been trained by a professional have a better chance of a first-time pass than those who are trained by a non-professional instructor, no matter how experienced a driver he or she may be.

The reason that professional training is almost invariably more successful than that given by even the most gifted of amateur teachers is twofold. First, any driving instructor worth his salt knows from experience what routes local examiners use and is able to instruct on either the same roads or on similar ones. Secondly, the instructor himself has trained for his job and has not developed those easy-going driving habits that are all too common in non-professionals.

The need constantly to maintain one's standards explains why so many keen drivers go on to submit themselves voluntarily to a far stiffer test – that conducted by the Institute of Advanced Motorists. This is a searching examination, based largely on police driving practices, and the quality of the test is matched by the quality of the examiners themselves. All hold the Police Class One driving certificate, and as far as road driving goes that means they are the best in Britain, and probably in the world.

It opens with a full briefing, lasting some 30 minutes. Then comes the actual driving over a route of approximately 35 miles, with motorway stretches included wherever possible, together with sections of typical town streets, busy dual carriageways, and country lanes. About 1 ½ hours are allowed for this. Then comes the part that every candidate probably rates as the most important of all – half an hour of debriefing, during which the examiner discusses the candidate's performance in detail. One can learn more about one's driving in that half-hour than in a thousand miles alone on the road and, pass or fail, that in itself makes the IAM test worth every penny it costs to take.

The Institute is based in London – at IAM House, 359 Chiswick High Road, London W4 4HS (081-994-4403/06) – but it has groups throughout the country, operating tests over 87 routes. These include eight in Scotland, five in Wales, and two in Northern Ireland.

On passing the test you are entitled to become a member of the Institute. Since there are insurance companies that offer preferential rates to drivers who have the IAM Certificate, this is one test that can actually pay for itself.

What can't be priced in mere money, however, is the fact – confirmed by the Transport and Road Research Laboratory – that when 2000 people who had passed the IAM test were subsequently assessed they were found to have 50 per cent safer records than drivers who had not taken it.

What better investment in your future can you make?

# First, the Test

Let's put it into perspective. The driving test, however formidable it may look to a learner, is not an end in itself. It does not even signal the end of your period as a novice. Instead, passing the test is only the beginning of a long process of gaining the skills and experience that mark out a truly skilled driver. And that is a life-long operation, in which the driving test is no more than the first milestone.

No book can tell you how to pass the test first time round, mainly because Britain's driving test is not an examination. It is an assessment, made by an individual examiner, of your ability to carry out safely a limited number of reasonably simple driving manoeuvres in the space of a mere 30 minutes. Combined with that is a rudimentary eyesight test, and after the road assessment you will be required to answer perhaps half a dozen questions on the contents of The Highway Code and identify up to six signs and road markings.

You can fail the test before you can even slide behind the wheel if you cannot read a car number plate at a distance of 67 feet (75 feet, if the letters are 3 ½ inches high instead of 3 ⅛ inches). You can fail by not reaching what the examiner regards as a satisfactory standard of safe and competent driving on any one or all of the road exercises. You can fail if you cannot give the right answers to his oral questions on the Code, which may be drawn from any part of that 76-page booklet. And the sad truth is that, despite the best efforts of skilled driving instructors to train folk to a standard at which failure is almost unthinkable, the failure rate in the elementary British driving test is a massive 53 per cent!

Curiously, this is one of the worst failure rates in the whole of Europe. Even in countries such as Austria or Germany, where the driving tests include night driving, motorway driving, parking – a curious omission in our test – and a written theory/literacy examination, the pass rate is 50 per cent or above. Only in Britain and Holland is the rate below 50 per cent, but the Dutch test includes motorway driving and parking, as well as skid recovery. Since there is no evidence that Continental driving instruction is inherently superior, or that foreign drivers are better than British, the only conclusion that can be drawn is that the venerable British test is at once too random and too arbitrary. Accept that disadvantage from the start, however, and you will be psychologically better equipped to ensure that you will be among the 47 per cent who pass first time.

But does that really matter? Obviously, your driving instructor will be grooming you with the test in mind and, as a professional, he will ensure that you are well prepared. Although enrolling with a first-class driving school cannot guarantee an instant pass, it certainly makes it more likely. What is more important is that you will be given a solid grounding in sound techniques that will stand you in good stead through the whole of your driving life, when the test itself has become only a hazy memory.

*Everybody* passes the test, some sooner, some later. So don't let it dominate your driving. Concentrate, instead, on the aim of becoming a skilled driver – a safe driver. The rest will follow.

## This is the test

The aim of the Department of Transport is to produce a test format that can be applied consistently throughout Britain – which, paradoxically, means that it cannot be exactly the same everywhere. London traffic conditions cannot be reproduced in the heart of Devon, and while it's easy enough to find sites for hill starts in the Highlands of Scotland it is not so simple in the Fens. Examiners – and candidates – have to take the ground as they find it, and though the same standards of judgement are applied nationally the actual content of the test itself may vary from area to area.

Generally, however, the practical test will follow much the same pattern. You will have with you your test card, giving the time and place of the test – this may have to be booked several months in advance in the busier centres – together with your provisional driving licence, your certificate of insurance and, where applicable, your car's MOT test certificate. Your car must carry a current tax disc and be completely roadworthy. These are essentials – and so is arrival at the test centre in good time. Each examiner works to a tight schedule, with up to eight tests to conduct each day, and lateness can mean that the test cannot be carried out.

When your test is due, the examiner will call your name and ask you to sign the attendance register – which also gives him the chance to check your signature against the application form. Attempts at impersonation are not unknown . . . Neither are pre-test nerves (for which he may make some allowance). However, if you have tried to quell them with a spot of Dutch courage in the local hostelry your test could end before it has begun, for the examiner has the right to refuse to accompany any candidate whom he believes to have taken alcohol.

Some candidates are excused, on medical grounds, from wearing seat belts. If you are one of them you should at this stage show your exemption certificate to the examiner.

Finally, you will be asked whether you suffer from any physical disability that has not been declared on your application form. This is simply to up-date his information, since the form may have been submitted several months earlier.

Formalities over, the test can now begin, and you will be asked to lead the way to your car, and to identify it to the examiner. Once he knows that he is not asking you to read your own numberplate the examiner will select a vehicle at random and ask you to tell him its number. Get it right and there's no problem. Get it wrong twice, and the examiner will measure out the statutory distance, using an official tape, and give you a third and final chance. Fail that and you've failed the whole test.

You can, of course, wear glasses when taking the eyesight test. If you do, however, then you must wear the same glasses throughout the rest of the test – as you would expect.

Now you will be invited to get into your car, where the examiner will join you shortly. He, meantime, will be walking round it, entering the necessary details of make and model on his driving test report sheet, and satisfying himself that the vehicle is roadworthy. If it isn't, he cannot continue the test. He'll be checking that there are no broken or missing lamp lenses; that the windscreen wipers are in place; that the tyres appear to be sound and that the treads comply with legal requirements; and that vision is not impaired. That could even extend to a dirty windscreen, so be warned.

You might think that nobody would turn up for a driving test in a car on which the requisite L-plates were not properly displayed. Wrong! People sometimes do, and find their tests abandoned as a consequence. The examiner is also entitled to refuse to carry out the test if the plates have been so positioned that they (or other stickers, or silly little swinging mascots) can obstruct vision from the driving seat. And he can call proceedings to a halt if, on entering the car, he finds that the seat belts are tangled, or dirty, or are damaged in such a way that they no longer comply with legal requirements.

He won't actually ask you to start the engine, though he will want to check the safety actions involved in a start-up – something that pilots call 'cockpit drill'. He will simply tell you that he wishes you to follow the road ahead unless traffic signs direct otherwise, or unless he asks you to turn. Then he indicates that you should move off when you are ready – and you are in for a busy 30 minutes.

This part of the driving test is concerned with your ability to carry out normal driving manoeuvres safely, apply the Highway Code in practice, and show other road users both care and consideration.

You will be asked to do some or all of these things: start up and move off; turns to left and right; pull in to the roadside; make an emergency stop; reverse into a limited opening, to the left or right; enter and leave a roundabout; restart on a gradient, up or down; turn in the road, using forward and reverse gears. In between, of course, your handling of the car in natural driving conditions will be assessed.

On your return to the test centre, you will be asked a number of questions on the Highway Code and related subjects. The first stage is to identify traffic signs – six in all. Since there are well over one hundred of them in the Code (and more still in the official *Know Your Traffic Signs* booklet, which is well worth studying) you can't hope to permutate. You'll simply have to learn them all . . .

Lastly you can expect to be asked a further six questions on the Code – again, drawn at random and not necessarily confined to the 'Road User on Wheels' section. Furthermore, you may have to answer questions about motorway driving – something that you, as a learner, have yet to experience. But that's not a subterfuge to keep you in L-plates: in theory, you may be free in a few minutes time to take those off and drive gaily down the M1 or entangle yourself on the M25, or join the queues on the M6. So the examiner may well wish to be sure that at least you've read up on the techniques.

This is the moment of truth. The examiner faces you and tells you that the test is over. Then – 'I'm pleased to tell you that you have passed.' Or, 'I'm sorry you haven't passed.'

Either way, you'll receive a certificate. The pass certificate has to be signed, and sent to the DVLC in Swansea, together with your provisional licence (which he will now want to see) which is surrendered when a substantive licence is issued.

Less welcome is the alternative 'Statement of Failure' form, on which the examiner will have marked those of the 20 matters 'needing special attention' that have led him to conclude that you are not yet ready to drive unsupervised.

There is no way that you will see his own marked driving test report sheet, nor will the examiner discuss either his decision or details of the test with you. You may not be alone in thinking that the cause of road safety would be better served by a more open and constructive approach – many examiners agree with you – but at least you can talk the results over with your own driving instructor, who understands what the DoT's terse shorthand comments imply.

Meantime, it's back to school – and applying for another driving test . . .

# The Code

There is no doubt whatsoever which book is the most vital to a learner driver – the Highway Code has no rivals, because without a thorough knowledge of its contents no learner can hope to pass the test. Indigestible as it looks at first glance, it is nevertheless indispensable and it has the merit of condensing a wealth of roadmanship into a remarkably small space.

Although it is an official publication it does not have the force of law behind it. You cannot be prosecuted for failing to obey the Code as such, but any failure on your part to adhere to its precepts *is* admissible as evidence of guilt.

For all these reasons a sensible road user, whether motorist, pedestrian or cyclist, is well advised to study it.

For you, as a learner, the major concern is obviously how the code can help you pass your test – and how seriously the lack of knowledge can hinder you.

The short answer to that one is that without a detailed knowledge of the Code it is impossible to pass the driving test. The oral examination is based upon it, and during the road section of the test the examiner will expect you to drive within both the spirit and letter of the Code. There is no short cut: you must study the Code itself and learn from it, though the following summary of some of its principal points can be used to refresh your memory. The Code opens with **advice to pedestrians** which have also particular relevance to drivers. Summarised, it advises:

Use a pavement or footpath if possible. Otherwise, walk facing oncoming traffic and as close to the side as possible. Place yourself between any children and traffic. Wear light-coloured or reflective clothing in darkness or poor light. When marching as a group, keep to the left: with lookouts at front and rear carrying, respectively,

16

white and red lights. The outer rank should carry additional lights and wear reflective clothing. Walking on motorways and their slip roads is forbidden. Observe the Green Cross Code when you wish to cross a highway. If there is an island, stop there and repeat the Green Cross Code sequence. Watch for turning traffic if crossing at a junction. Use a zebra crossing if possible, but avoid the area marked with zigzag lines. At zebras, give drivers and cyclists time to slow: traffic does not have to stop until you have stepped on to the crossing. Keep looking both ways when crossing over. A crossing divided by an island is two crossings, not one. At pelican crossings controlled by traffic lights do not cross when the 'red man' signal is showing. Cross when the steady 'green man' signal appears. Do not start to cross if the 'green man' signal is flashing. A pelican which goes straight across the road is one crossing even if there is an island. But if the crossing is staggered each half is a separate light-controlled crossing. Obey pedestrian signals at normal traffic lights, watching for turning traffic. At crossings controlled by police, wardens, or patrols, await their signals and cross only in front of them. Don't climb guard rails – use the gaps. In one-way streets check the traffic flow direction and use the Green Cross Code. Apply this also when crossing bus lanes. Avoid crossing where vehicles are parked or in front of any vehicle whose engine is running. At night, cross near a street light. Do not cross a road being used by emergency vehicles. Board and alight from a bus only when it is standing at a stop; never cross behind or in front of one, but wait until it moves off. And take great care at level crossings.

Next, the Code deals with **road users on wheels**. It opens this section with general advice:

Check your vehicle's condition – lights, brakes, steering, all tyres, belts, demisters, wipers and washers. Clean screens, windows, lenses, indicators, reflectors, plates. Don't drive if the exhaust system is faulty or unsuitable. L-plates should be covered or removed if the car is not being used for instruction or practice. Ensure that any loads carried or towed are secure and not projecting unsafely. Don't overload. If you are tired or ill, or under the influence of drugs of medicines, don't drive. Check prescriptions with your doctor. Spectacles must be worn if they are needed to meet the official eyesight standard. Don't use tinted glasses at night or in poor visibility – and don't use tinted materials or sprays on car screens or windows.

On alcohol, the Code warns that the risk of an accident increases sharply above the legal limit of 35 microgrammes of alcohol per 100 millilitres of breath, and that the driving of people who feel sober is often affected well below that limit, since drink reduces co-ordination, increases reaction times, impairs judgement of speed, distance and risk, and instils a false sense of confidence. Don't drink and drive.

On seat belts, it draws attention to the law requiring their use by drivers and front-seat passengers (except those who have a medical exemption certificate; are executing a manoeuvre that includes reversing; or are making local rounds of collection or delivery in a vehicle adapted for the purpose). Ensuring that children under 14 are suitably restrained if travelling in the front is the driver's responsibility. Young children should wear an approved child restraint and travel in the rear – but not in the luggage space of an estate car or hatchback. Child safety doorlocks, where fitted, should be secured.

On **signs and signals**, the Code says:

Know and act on traffic signs and road markings. Give signals if they can help or warn others, but give only the correct signals and do so in good time and clearly. Always check afterwards that your indicators have cancelled. Watch for other people's signals and act accordingly. Obey all signals given by police or wardens controlling traffic, and by school crossing patrols.

Advice on **moving off and driving along** includes these points:

Always use mirrors before moving off, but as a final check look round too. If necessary, signal before pulling out, and move off only if it can be done safely and without causing other road users to alter speed or direction.

Keep to the left unless signs or markings indicate otherwise, or if you are going to overtake, turn right, or pass stationary traffic or pedestrians. Let others overtake you. Never drive on a footpath or pavement. Make frequent use of your mirrors to check traffic behind or on either side. Use the mirrors and if necessary give the appropriate signal before overtaking, stopping, slowing or turning either to left or right. Always observe the 'mirrors – signal – manoeuvre' routine. Two-wheeled vehicles are not easy to see; keep a special watch for them, particularly when overtaking or turning. When driving long distances, ensure plenty of ventilation to keep you alert, and if you feel tired stop at a suitable parking place to rest. Obey all speed limits: except on motorways, a 30mph limit is in force wherever there are street lights unless signs show a different limit. If conditions require, drive below the limit – it is a maximum, and not necessarily a safe speed. Always drive so that you can stop well within the distance you can see to be clear, reducing speed if the road is wet or icy, in fog, and at night. Brake sharply only in emergencies. Always leave enough clearance between your vehicle and that in front so that you can stop safely if it slows or pulls up suddenly. The recommended safe minimum gap is 12m at 20mph, 23m at 30mph, 36m at 40mph, 53m at 50mph, 73m at 60mph, and 96m at 70mph. On open roads in good conditions, one metre per mph of speed or a two-second time gap may suffice. Clearances should be doubled on wet or icy roads. If an overtaking vehicle pulls in ahead, drop back to restore clearance.

Make way for ambulances, fire engines, police or other emergency vehicles, flashing blue lights or sounding bells, duo-tone horns and sirens. Where it is safe to do so, give way to buses indicating an intention to move off from stops in towns. When moving, don't use handheld microphones or phone handsets; speak into a retained microphone only if doing so does not distract your attention from the road; and don't stop on a motorway hard shoulder to make or answer calls.

In fog, check the mirrors – then slow so that you can pull up within your range of vision. Maintain adequate clearance and never try to follow another vehicle's tail lights. Check your speed. Don't try to accelerate away from a vehicle close behind. Observe and obey warning signals. Use dipped headlamps or front fog lamps so you can see and be seen. Use rear fog lamps only in seriously reduced visibility (less than 100m). Operate wipers and demisters. Wherever possible, check and clean screens, windows, lights and reflectors. Don't be misled by an apparent clearance – fog drifts, and can thicken suddenly. Particular care is needed in fog after dark. If you must drive in fog, allow more time for the trip.

The Code emphasises a driver's duty of **care for the safety of pedestrians**:

When pedestrians are about drive slowly and carefully. Pay particular attention in crowded shopping streets, near a stopped bus or a parked milk float or mobile shop. Pedestrians may step suddenly from behind vehicles that are stopped or parked. Show consideration to pedestrians crossing roads where there are no zebra or pelican crossings. Watch particularly for the young and the old – their judgement of speed may be faulty. Allow plenty of time for blind people (they may carry white sticks) or the deaf/blind (white stick with two red reflectorised bands) or with guide dogs. The deaf may not have heard your approach.

Near schools, drive slowly and watch for pupils boarding or

alighting from buses. Stop when signalled to do so by a school crossing patrol. A place of particular danger is sometimes indicated by a flashing amber light under the advance warning sign indicating that a school crossing patrol is ahead. Special care is needed near a parked ice-cream van. When approaching a pedestrian crossing look for people waiting to cross; be prepared to slow or stop to allow them to do so. You must give way to anybody who has stepped on to a zebra crossing: signal to other drivers that you intend to slow or stop, and allow extra distance for stopping if the road is wet or icy. Never signal pedestrians to cross: another vehicle may be approaching.

Never overtake on the approach to a zebra crossing. Where the crossing has zigzag lines on the approach, you must not overtake the vehicle nearest the crossing, or the leading vehicle that has stopped to give way to a pedestrian. In traffic queues, leave zebra crossing clear. Where a pedestrian crossing is controlled by lights, a police officer, or a warden, give way to pedestrians still crossing when the signal allows vehicles to move.

Signals at pelican crossings have the same meaning as at traffic lights, but the red stop signal is followed by a flashing amber light. While this operates, vehicles must give way to any pedestrian still on the crossing. On a straight crossing, even if there is an island, vehicles must wait for pedestrians crossing from the further side of the refuge.

Give way to pedestrians who, at road junctions, are crossing the road into which you are turning. Give way to pedestrians when you are entering or leaving a property bordering on a road. Give way also to other traffic. On roads with no footpaths, allow ample room when passing pedestrians, marches, or processions, and reduce speed; left-hand bends demand special care. This also applies to animals being led – drive slowly, allow plenty of room, and do not frighten them by use of the horn or high engine speeds.

When it comes to **overtaking**, the Code again stresses the importance to safe driving of the 'mirrors-signal-manoeuvre' routine, and advises:

Never overtake unless you are sure it can be done without danger to yourself and others. The road ahead must be clear far enough ahead and behind. Use mirrors, and signal before you begin to move out. Remember that it's more difficult to judge both speed and distance at dusk, or when it is dark, foggy, or misty. Also, vehicles behind may be overhauling you faster than you may think. Allow the vehicle you are overtaking ample room, pass it quickly, and regain the left-hand side of the road as soon as possible. Do not, however, cut in. Give extra room when passing motorcycles, cyclists, or equestrians; pass none of them if you intend to make an immediate left turn.

With only four exceptions, all overtaking must be done on the right. The exceptions are: when the vehicle in front has indicated a right turn and it is possible to overtake on its left without impeding other traffic or entering an operative bus lane; if you yourself intend to turn left at a junction, or to park – lane changes for overtaking are inadmissible; or if, in slow-moving traffic queues, vehicles in the lane to your right are moving more slowly than you; or in one-way streets, where vehicles may pass on either side. Note that this does *not* apply to dual carriageways.

When being overtaken, either keep a steady speed or slow down to let the other vehicle pass. If, on a two-lane road, you need to move out to the right to pass parked vehicles or a road obstruction, give way to any vehicle that is coming towards you *before* you pull out. You must not overtake if to do so entails crossing or straddling a double white line road marking where the solid line is nearer to you, nor within the zigzag lined area on the approach to a zebra crossing; nor before the end of a restriction after passing a 'No overtaking' sign. If you are approaching an area where you cannot see far enough ahead to be certain that overtaking is safe – the Code instances corners, bends, hump-backed bridges or the brow of hills – overtaking should not be commenced. Do not overtake where there is a danger of coming into conflict with other road users – examples are road junctions, level crossings, points at which a road narrows, or where you would have to drive over an area marked with diagonal stripes or chevrons. Do not overtake when doing so would cause another vehicle to swerve or to slow down. If you have any doubt, do not overtake . . .

The Code's section on **road junctions** opens on a cautionary note: Approach with care: check your position and speed, and drive on only when it is safe to do so. Don't block the junction. Watch for long vehicles turning to left or right – they may need the whole road width. Beware of cyclists, motorcyclists, and pedestrians waiting to cross. Don't assume, when waiting at a junction, that a vehicle coming from the right with its left indicator operating will in fact turn left: wait till you are sure.

Where the junction is marked by double broken lines across the road you must allow traffic on the major road to go by first. Such a junction may also have the words 'Give way' on the carriageway, or an inverted triangle. Where, however, there is a 'Stop' sign and a solid white line you *must* pull up at the line and wait for a safe gap in the traffic before moving off. Treat each half of a dual carriageway as a separate road. If the central reservation is at least as wide as your vehicle's length, cross into the gap and wait until there is a safe gap in the traffic on the other carriageway. Then cross, or turn right, as appropriate. Where the central reservation is narrow, and your car would project into either carriageway, remain stationary until you can safely cross the whole road in one movement. Crisscross yellow lines on the road mark a box junction, which you may not enter unless your exit is clear – except to turn right. At junctions controlled by police or wardens, wait for the officer's signal before filtering left or right. At light-controlled junctions, go forward only on the green and then only if there is room for you to clear the whole junction safely. Where the traffic signals have a filter arrow, enter the filter lane only if you wish to follow it. Allow room for other road users to move into their proper lanes. At all light-controlled junctions, wait behind the solid white 'Stop' line if halted. When turning, look for and give room to cyclists, motorcyclists and pedestrians.

To turn right, check in your mirrors, well beforehand, what following traffic is doing. Then, once you are certain it is safe, signal a right turn and move to a position just left of centre of the road, or into the space marked for traffic turning right. If possible, leave room for others to pass to your left. Wait for a safe gap in oncoming traffic, look out for cyclists, motorcyclists and pedestrians, and make your turn without cutting the corner.

When turning right at a junction where an oncoming vehicle is also turning right, position yourself with the other car on your right-hand side so that you pass offside to offside. Pass nearside to nearside (other vehicle on your left) only if the junction layout makes the preferred offside passing impractical, or if road markings or the position of the other vehicle make it necessary. In both cases, check for traffic on the carriageway you want to cross, remembering that in a nearside pass it may be masked by the other vehicle.

To turn left, check in your mirrors well in advance, then signal a left turn. Both before and after, keep well to the left – safety, and your car length, are limiting factors – and remember to give way to pedestrians crossing the road into which you are turning. Look out for two-wheelers and do not overtake them before your proposed turn. Watch for other vehicles and bicycles using any bus lane you have to cross.

Some junctions have mini roundabouts. Here, the normal rules for **roundabouts** apply. On approach, note vehicles already on the roundabout and give way to traffic on your right unless road markings indicate otherwise. Keep moving if it's clear, but watch for 'Give way' lines. Unless road markings indicate otherwise, when turning left from a roundabout approached by two lanes keep in the left-hand lane throughout. When going straight on – unless road conditions dictate otherwise, when it is permissible to use the right-hand lane – approach on the left, keep to the left in the roundabout, and exit left. On a clear roundabout take the most convenient route. When turning right, use the right-hand lane on the approach and in the roundabout.

The signals to be given at roundabouts are: When turning left, indicate left on the approach and through the roundabout. When going straight on, indicate left when you pass the exit before the one you wish to take. When turning right, indicate right on the approach and through the roundabout as far as the exit before the one you intend to take: then indicate left. In all cases watch for cyclists and motorcyclists, and for long vehicles that may need to take a different course to negotiate the roundabout.

The Code gives three pieces of advice on **reversing**: Before reversing, ensure that no pedestrians – particularly children – or obstructions are behind you: check the 'blind' area you cannot see from the driving seat. If you cannot see clearly behind, ask somebody to guide you back. Never reverse into a main road from a side road, and keep all reversing as short as you can.

**Lamps** come next. The Code says:

Make sure all lamps are clean and working, and that headlamps are properly adjusted to prevent dazzle. Switch on at lighting-up time, using headlamps at night on all roads without street lamps, or where they are 200 yards (185 m) or more apart, or where they aren't lit. In visibility of less than 100m, use headlamps or front fog lamps. Use rear fog lamps *only* under those conditions, not because there is rain, mist or darkness. Headlamps should be used at night on lighted motorways and other high-speed roads. In built-up areas, except where well lit, use dipped headlamps. Drive so you can stop well within the distance you can see ahead. If dazzled, slow down or stop. Dip your lights early when meeting other vehicles, either ahead of you or approaching.

Use headlamp flashing only as a warning of approach. Never use the horn except as a warning. It must not be sounded on a moving vehicle between 11.30 pm and 7 am in built-up areas. When stationary, sound the horn only if there is danger from a moving vehicle.

A dozen prohibitions open the Code's section on **waiting and parking**. No vehicle is allowed to stand:

On a motorway, except (in an emergency) on the hard shoulder. On any pedestrian crossing; in the area either side of a zebra that's marked with zigzag lines, or in the approach zone of a pelican that's marked by studs, except when allowing a pedestrian to cross. On the right-hand side of a carriageway (except in a one-way street) at night. On a clearway, except in an emergency; on an urban clearway (or its verges) during times indicated on the signs, for longer than it takes passengers to board or alight. On a bus lane or cycle lane (during operative times) except where it is permitted to load or unload goods. On the carriageway or verges of a road where there are double white lines, even if one is broken, except to allow passengers to board or alight, or to load or unload goods. On the side of the carriageway, or on the pavement or verge, marked by yellow lines during the times given on the plates on that side of the road – again, except for passengers to board or alight, or goods to be loaded or unloaded. Time plates are put up in controlled parking zones only where restricted times differ from those on the entry signs. Loading and unloading are not permitted during times shown on a 'No loading' plate where there are kerb marks: and the absence of yellow lines does not indicate that parking is necessarily permitted. There may be concessions for the disabled.

A vehicle parked in a disc zone must display a parking disc – operating times and parking periods appear on roadside plates and entry signs.

Parking in places reserved for specific users is restricted to those users. There is no parking between 7am and 7pm at bus stops marked by wide yellow lines (authorised buses and coaches are exempt). Goods vehicles whose maximum laden weight, including trailer, exceeds 7.5 tonnes are banned from any verge, central reservation or footway save in certain specified circumstances.

In addition, no vehicle must stand where it would cause danger to other road users, including pedestrians. Examples include: at or near a school entrance or a crossing patrol; hiding a traffic sign; at or near a bus stop or level crossing.

Parking must not obstruct sight lines – not within 15m of a junction, not on a bend or the brow of a hill, or a humpback bridge. The road must not be narrowed by parking opposite a traffic island, alongside another stationary vehicle, or opposite or nearly opposite one if the road is then narrowed to less than the width of two vehicles; or near road works.

Parking must not hold up or inconvenience traffic – examples given include on narrow roads, fly-overs, tunnels, underpasses, fast main roads except in lay-bys, on single-tracks roads or their passing places, blocking vehicle access to properties or the entrance or exit of a car park, or in a way that would prevent the use of properly parked vehicles.

There must be no waiting or parking where emergency vehicles operate or stop – at hospital and ambulance entrances, doctors' entrances, police and fire stations, by fire hydrants, or at entrances to coastguard stations.

Parking, in general, must be safe and must cause the least inconvenience to others. Always use off-road parking where possible.

A hazard warning device on a vehicle must not be used as an excuse to stop where it is not permitted: it can only be operated when the vehicle is stationary to indicate a temporary obstruction, as in a breakdown or during loading or unloading.

Before opening any door, check that nobody on the road or footpath is close enough to be hit by it – again, the Code urges particularly that you must watch for cyclists and motorcyclists. Driver and passengers should alight on the side nearer the kerb wherever possible.

When parking on the road, stop as close to the edge as possible, and before leaving check that the handbrake is firmly on, the engine and headlamps switched off, and the vehicle locked. Avoid parking on the road at night, or in fog. Vehicles that are parked under these conditions must always display lights, but those under 1525kg unladen may be parked without lights on a road subject to a limit of 30mph or less if the vehicle is at least 10m clear of a junction, is close to and parallel to the kerb, and faces the direction of the traffic flow. Alternatively, it must be in a recognised parking place. Exemption does not apply to trailers or to vehicles whose loads project.

On **breakdowns and accidents** the Code's advice is:

If you break down, think first of other traffic; get your vehicle off the road if possible; keep yourself and your passengers off the road. Warn other drivers – use hazard warning lights, and place a reflective red triangle at least 50m before the obstruction. On motorway hard shoulders, position it 150m distant. If warning cones are available, place the first one 15m from the obstruction and next to the kerb, and the last level with the outside of the obstruction. At night or in poor visibility don't obscure the rear lamps by allowing anybody to stand at the rear of the vehicle.

On roads other than motorways, if anything falls from your vehicle, stop as soon as safety allows and remove it from the carriageway.

An accident ahead may be recognisable by seeing several distant vehicles moving slowly or stopped, or by warning signs, or flashing lights on emergency vehicles. Slow, and be ready to stop. If first on the scene at an accident, warn other traffic by using hazard warning lights, warning triangles, cones, or any other safe means. Don't smoke, and ensure that all drivers switch off their engines. Call police and ambulance services immediately (on a motorway, drive on to the next emergency phone) giving exact location and casualties. Remove any casualty who is in further immediate danger, but only where necessary. Give first aid. Direct uninjured people to safety – away from the carriageway, hard shoulder or central reservation on motorways. Stay on the scene until emergency services arrive.

If a vehicle involved contained dangerous goods (a hazard information panel may be displayed) pass details to the police or fire brigade, and keep everybody well away from it. Be cautious even if saving lives – there may be dangerous liquids, dust, or vapours.

Special advice on **motorway driving** is contained in the Code:

Motorways must not be used by pedestrians, learner drivers, cyclists, riders of small motorcycles, slow-moving vehicles, agricultural machinery, or some invalid carriages. Passengers or hitch-hikers must not be picked up on motorways or slip roads.

As traffic travels faster than on ordinary roads, situations must be summed up quickly. Use mirrors and constant concentration.

Ensure your vehicle is fit to cruise at speed. Set the correct M-way tyre pressures, and have sufficient fuel, oil and water to reach at least the nearest service area. Any loads carried or towed must be secure. Reduce speed on slip roads and link roads – they may have sharp bends. When joining a motorway from a slip road give way to traffic already on the motorway; watch for a safe gap in the flow in the left-hand lane and adjust your speed to match in the acceleration lane. Wait in the acceleration lane if there is no suitable gap; join the motorway only when it is safe to do so. After joining, stay in the left-hand lane and get used to the speeds before moving out to overtake.

While on a motorway, you must not reverse, turn in the road, cross the central reservation, or drive against the traffic. If you miss a turn-off, or are on the wrong route, carry on until the next exit. Drive at a steady speed within the limits of your vehicle, appropriate to visibility and weather. Don't exceed speed limits. Reduce speed in the wet, on ice, or in fog. If you feel sleepy, let fresh air into the vehicle, stop at a service area (or take an exit) and then walk a little.

On two-lane carriageways, drive in the left-hand lane unless overtaking. With three or more lanes this rule still applies – though you may stay in the middle lane when there are slower vehicles in the left-hand lane. Return to it after passing them. The right-hand lane is for overtaking only; move back to the middle lane, then to the left-hand lane, as soon as possible after passing but without cutting in.

The carriageway's right-hand edge is marked by amber studs; the left-hand edge by red studs; the green studs separate the acceleration and deceleration lanes from the carriageway.

Watch for direction signs placed over the road; move into the right lane in good time. Goods vehicles above 7.5 tonnes, vehicles drawing caravans or trailers, or buses longer than 12 metres are barred from the right-hand lane on motorways with three lanes or more, but they may use them in exceptional circumstances.

In fog on motorways, apply the advice already given for normal roads.

Overtake only on the right; never move to a lane on the left, or on to the hard shoulder, to pass. If traffic is moving in queues, and that to your right is slower-moving, you may pass it. Don't risk rear-end collisions – before overtaking, make sure that the lane you wish to join is clear for sufficient distance *behind* you, as well as ahead; follow the 'mirror-signal-manoeuvre' routine, and take particular care at dusk, in the dark, in fog, or in mist.

Return to the left-hand lane (middle lane if appropriate) without cutting in, but as soon as you reasonably can.

**Motorway breakdowns** are particularly hazardous, and the Code gives specific advice.

Pull off the carriageway and as far to the left of the hard shoulder as possible. Minimise danger from passing traffic by switching on hazard warning lights and, at night, sidelights too. Use the doors farther from the carriageway. Don't stand behind the car, or between it and the traffic. Use the nearest emergency telephone on your side – never try to cross the motorway to use those on the other side. Motorway marker posts carry arrows indicating the nearest phone. Return to your car as soon as you can – don't leave it unattended for longer than necessary. If you have been forced to stop on the carriageway itself, use hazard warning lights and a reflective triangle placed 150m on the approach side (and cones if possible) to warn approaching traffic.

It is up to you to decide whether passengers should remain in the vehicle. If they leave it, they must not stand behind it or wander on the hard shoulder. Keep children under strict control; leave animals in the vehicle. On restarting, gain speed on the hard shoulder and watch for a safe gap before rejoining the left-hand lane.

Don't try to retrieve anything that has fallen from your vehicle or another; inform the police, using an emergency telephone.

There are special rules governing **stopping and parking** on motorways.

You *must not* stop except in an emergency, if your vehicle breaks down, or if the police, emergency traffic signs or flashing red lights require you to do so. Parking is permitted *only* at a service area: *not* on the carriageway, the slip roads, the central reservation or (save in emergency) the hard shoulder. And you must never walk on the carriageway, or let children or animals free on carriageways or the hard shoulder.

At **roadworks** on motorways, the Code requires:

Exercise special care, observing signs, signals and speed limits. Check in mirrors, join the appropriate lane early and adjust your speed. Maintain a safe clearance from the vehicle ahead.

When **leaving the motorway**:

If leaving by a slip road, watch for the signs and be in the left-hand lane well before the turn-off point. Stay in it, signal a left-hand turn in good time, reduce speed if necessary. Join the acceleration lane, and slow down before taking the slip road. After leaving the motorway or link road, adjust your driving to the new conditions and make speedometer checks – your speed will be higher than you think.

# Road Signs and Markings

Most, if not all, **road signs and markings** a driver will commonly
encounter are illustrated in the Highway Code. You need to learn
them all.

**Mandatory signs** – those that give orders – are normally circular,
and those bordered by a red circle are mostly prohibitions. They
include those indicating statutory speed limits (except the white
sign with black diagonal bar, often wrongly called 'the deregulation
sign') that indicates that the national speed limit of 70mph on
motorways and dual carriageways, or 60mph elsewhere, applies.
Examples of other mandatory signs are those prohibiting entry to
vehicular traffic; those instructing that priority must be given to
approaching vehicles; weight, width or height restrictions, and the
sign prohibiting stopping on clearways. Two notable exceptions are
the red hexagonal 'Stop' sign (at which you must stop and give way)
and the red-bordered inverted triangle of the 'Give way' sign,
indicating that you must give way to traffic on the major road.

Oblong signs that are mandatory include those restricting parking to classes of people named on the sign, and the urban clearway
sign. In addition, the messages conveyed by other signs may be
modified by instructions carried in an oblong white plate below the
sign itself.

Also mandatory, of course, are the light signals controlling
traffic. The 'red, amber, green' traffic lights are both familiar and
unequivocal – which doesn't mean they are always properly
interpreted.

In fact, in the normal sequence – red, red and amber, green,
amber, red – all except the green light actually require you to stop,
and even green gives only a qualified permission to go.

A single red light means that you are obliged to stop and wait behind the white stop line painted on the carriageway.

Red and amber together also mean that you must stop and remain stationary until the green light shows.

Green signifies that you may go *providing* the way ahead is clear. But, if you are turning to left or right and pedestrians are crossing the carriageway into which you intend to turn, then the way is *not* clear and you must allow them to regain the footpath before proceeding.

Amber alone requires you to stop at the stop line. The only exception to this is if you had already crossed the line when the amber light appeared, or if you were so close to it that to pull up might cause an accident. This illustrates the importance of always checking in the mirrors on the approach to traffic lights, so that you know precisely how far behind you the next vehicle is. It also indicates the importance of reducing speed on the approach, so that you can stop if required to do so. And stop you must – on amber, if you can; on red, as a matter of course.

Some traffic lights have, in addition to the three-lamp sequence, a supplementary display beside the green – an arrow. When this shows, movement in that direction is permitted whatever the other lights indicate – but again with the proviso that the way must be clear. Frequently, a separate filter lane is provided where lights of this type operate. Otherwise, they control a left-hand or right-hand lane open to traffic going straight ahead and to traffic turning. It is a courtesy for through traffic to leave that lane free for turning-off if possible.

Twin flashing red lights, usually accompanied by a steady amber light, are used at railway level crossings. You may also find them in a few other locations, such as airfields where the highway passes close to the end of the runway in use, at lifting bridges, and at fire stations and points to which emergency services require unimpeded access.

Whether associated with a lifting barrier or not, the operating sequence is the same. First, the amber lights up and there will usually also be an audible warning. Again, the amber phases means that you should stop, just as with ordinary traffic lights. Next, the red lights start to flash and the barriers operate. By then you should be at a standstill. Where they are guarding a railway crossing they may continue to flash once the train has passed. That means another train is coming.

On minor roads, half-barriers are sometimes used, blocking only the lefthand side of the road. Again, the amber lamp will light, the audible warning will sound, and the red lights will flash. Stop – and stay stopped – until the barrier lifts.

There may be a temptation to zigzag round the barrier. Resist it! These systems are automatic, operated by the approaching train itself. At best, the train is only half a mile away and travelling at a speed that will ensure that it will reach the crossing long before you could complete the maneouvre. It *couldn't* stop – a train's emergency stop is measured almost in miles, not yards – and any argument between a puny car and a heavy train is strictly no contest.

Some signs give a **positive instruction**. These are blue and lack a red border. Most are circular, though a few are oblong.

Examples of the circular sign include traffic directions – ahead only, turn right or left, left turn ahead, keep left or right, pass either side. Less common is a minimum speed sign and its cancellation. Bus and cycle lanes are examples of areas marked with blue oblongs.

Most **warning signs** – the most numerous group – appear as red-bordered triangles (stop and give way signs are inverted) with extra information carried on a white or red plate set below when the warning conveyed by the symbols requires to be more specific. The Highway Code illustrates over 40 examples, from crossroads and T-junctions to quaysides and low-flying aircraft, though one that may be encountered – the windsock symbol, indicating danger from side winds – is omitted. In the oral part of the driving test you can expect to be asked to identify up to six of these signs, so there's nothing for it but to learn all of them. A sensible precaution, since safe use of the roads depends on instant recognition of a sign and its message.

Signs relating to **direction** are mostly rectangular. On motorways, they have blue backgrounds; on primary routes, green backgrounds; on non-primary routes they are white with black borders. Most local direction signs are white with blue borders. They are self-explanatory, with a minimum use of symbols and a maximum reliance on plain English, complemented in some areas with Welsh.

The start of a motorway is indicated by a blue sign bearing the motorway symbol and its number; the end of a motorway by a blue sign with a red cancelling diagonal bar over the symbol. Motorways also have white marker posts set at 100m intervals along the far edge of the hard shoulder, with orange emergency telephones at mile intervals.

All information signs are rectangular, with blue, white, or yellow backgrounds. They mark entrances to controlled parking zones (there is a separate end-of-zone sign), indicate appropriate traffic lanes, one-way streets, permanent and temporary lane closures, bus lanes, and so on.

## Motorway signals

Some forms of signal are used only on motorways. Placed either on the central reservation at intervals of not more than two miles (or on overhead gantries where the road is a particularly busy one) they remain blank until conditions are dangerous. They are then lighted, and flashing amber lamps are activated, to display a temporary maximum speed limit or indicate which lanes are closed. At the end of the restriction a lighted form of the national speed limit sign is displayed. This is the 'end of restriction' signal.

Signs in the central reservation apply to all lanes of the motorway. Overhead signals are individual to each lane, and they are able to give more specific instructions. A numeral accompanied by flashing amber lights indicates a temporary speed restriction. A diagonal arrow with flashing amber lights requires drivers to change lane. A 'dog-leg' arrow with flashing amber lights instructs traffic to leave the motorway at the next exit. Flashing red lights mean that traffic should proceed no further in the lane over which they are displayed. When dangerous conditions no longer apply, the 'end of restriction' signal is exhibited.

Flashing red lights may also be applied to motorway slip roads. If they are operating, traffic must not enter the slip road.

On some motorways the older twin flashing amber light signals may still be encountered. They are placed at the motorway entrance and subsequently at intervals of one mile or two miles. They are activated to warn of danger – fog, an accident, or a risk of skidding. When these signals are operating, drivers should slow to a speed of less than 30mph until they are sure it is safe to exceed it.

The Code illustrates five types of **road marking** you will find across the carriageway, and six that are applied along it.

The first group all instruct you that you must either stop or give way. At a 'Stop' sign, a single broad solid line denotes the point at which you *must* pull up. It is an offence to trickle across it without stopping, even if you can see that the road is clear. A thinner solid white line is used in conjunction with traffic signals or where a junction is controlled by police, but the message is the same – you must stop unless you are signalled to do otherwise.

Markings indicating that you must give way have broken lines. Double broken lines at a junction indicate that you must give way to traffic on the major road. A single broken line composed of long white dashes indicates that you are about to enter a roundabout and that you must give way to traffic from the right. At a mini-roundabout the same message is conveyed by a broken line composed of much shorter dashes, closely spaced.

Included in the second group are some of the most important markings of all – double white lines along the carriageway. Two solid white lines are a prohibition. You *must not* cross or straddle the line that is nearest to you except in three instances set out in the Code. These are explicit:

1.   When you need to enter or leave premises or a side road.
2.   When ordered to do so by a police officer or a traffic warden.
3.   To avoid a *stationary* obstruction.

You could cross, therefore, to avoid a broken-down lorry but if the same lorry was limping along a few miles an hour with a failing engine you would commit a serious offence were you to cross the nearest line in order to overtake it. The same applies if you want to leave extra space when overtaking a cyclist, or a horse, or anything else that is slow-moving. The line must never be crossed, even if you can see that the road ahead is clear for miles.

In the case of a double white line system comprising one solid and one broken line you can cross them to overtake only if the broken line is on your side of the carriageway and you are certain that overtaking is not only safe, but can be completed before you reach a solid line on your side. If in doubt, hold back. Where the solid line is on your side, you must not cross or straddle it. On the line is out!

Usually the highway authority places white arrows ahead of a white line system to forewarn traffic of a restriction.

Even experienced drivers tend to misunderstand the third type of marking – diagonal stripes or chevrons bordered by solid or broken white lines. Frankly, these are one of the less sensible ideas dreamed up by the Department of Transport. The intention is laudable enough – to separate traffic streams liable to be a danger to each other or to protect traffic turning right. Fine in theory, but in practice they have the counter-productive effect of taking a carriageway of ample width and reducing it to a bottleneck that can result in tailbacks up to a mile long while the drivers at the front sort out a pecking order. The resulting frustration is likely to create more dangers than the system prevents . . .

As a driver, though, you will have to live with such nonsenses and as a candidate for the driving test you must understand their purpose and what is required of you when you encounter them. You *can* drive across them (but only if you cannot avoid doing so) providing the chevrons are bordered by a broken white line. Where the line is solid, you can enter the striped area only in an emergency.

The third group of markings, by contrast, is unquestionably helpful. These lane markings, centre lines, and hazard warning lines. Lane lines consist of widely-spaced short dashes dividing the carriageway into a number of lanes. There may also be road studs – cat's eyes – as a night-time guide. If so, the lanes will be marked by white studs (also used for road centre lines); the edge of the carriageway by red studs; the central reservation of a dual carriageway by amber studs. Lay-bys and the entrances to side roads may have green studs.

Where a road has lanes, proper lane discipline should be observed. Keep to the left-hand lane except when you wish to overtake or to pass a stationary vehicle. Then return to it. If you wish to turn right, move into the outer lane in good time. In all cases remember to observe the 'mirror-signal-manoeuvre' routine, and do not cause other drivers to slow down or swerve.

Avoid any unnecessary lane changes – those include switching from lane to lane to overtake in traffic hold-ups.

Some single-carriageway roads have only three lanes. On these, the outer lanes carry traffic travelling in different directions, and the centre lane is for overtaking and turning right. On such roads, that is the *only* purpose of the middle lane. Great care is needed when using it for overtaking, since oncoming traffic has exactly the same right to be there as you. At 60mph your joint speeds combine to give a closing speed of 120mph (176 feet per second!) which is a situation best avoided. A single engine misfire could mean big trouble, so restrict overtaking on three-lane roads to those times when oncoming traffic is sparse, and well spaced out. And it goes without saying that if you are using the outside lane then you should also be aware of what is coming the other way.

Some single-carriageway roads have four lanes. Look upon these as a form of dual carriageway (though one with the same 60mph restriction as single-carriageway roads) and use only the two lanes on the left-hand side – one for driving, one for overtaking – unless signs and road markings indicate you may do otherwise.

On dual carriageways, again, the left-hand lane is the one you should normally use, reserving the outer lane for overtaking or turning right. Where there are three lanes in each direction the middle lane can be used when there are slower vehicles in the left-hand lane. Return to the left when you have passed them. Again, the outer lane is for overtaking and right turns only. After overtaking, move back first into the middle lane, then into the left-hand lane, but without cutting in.

You will also find lanes in one-way streets. Select whichever is appropriate for the exit you plan to take – the left-hand lane if you propose to turn left, the right-hand lane for right turns. Choose your lane early and unless there are signs or road markings to the contrary stay in it. Where there are three lanes you may find vehicles passing on either side.

Where a single-carriageway road has only two lanes, one in each direction, it is usually divided in the centre by long, broken, white lines. Keep well to the left of the line unless you need to cross it to overtake, or intend to turn right.

Lastly, advance warning of a hazard – perhaps a sharp bend or a humpback bridge – is given by a single broken white line, the long dashes interspersed with short gaps. Adjust your speed accordingly, and do not cross the line unless you can see that the road ahead is clear well ahead.

Other road markings that you can expect to meet – and therefore must know – include the white inverted triangle on the carriageway that warns of a 'Give way' sign just ahead; the familiar black and white stripes of a zebra crossing where traffic *must* give way to any pedestrian who is on it; the zigzag white lines on each side of the crossing that prohibit overtaking or parking; reserved parking spaces marked by a box of broken white lines and the appellation of those entitled to use it; the instruction 'Keep clear' in large white letters intended (often unsuccessfully!) to prevent traffic blockage of side roads; and direction indications that help traffic to pass smoothly through towns and along unfamiliar routes.

Bus stops are clearly marked by a box of broken white lines and the words 'Bus Stop' in large white letters, and bus lanes by a solid white line and the words 'Bus Lane' in white capitals on the carriageway. These lanes may be in permanent operation. If they are not, there will be time plates on roadside signs, designating the hours during which only permitted vehicles (also specified on the signs) may enter the restricted lane. There are similar markings for cycle lanes – but don't confuse the two. You may be able to enter the bus lane during non-operational hours, but where a cycle lane has a solid line it is an offence either to drive on it or to park on it. Where a broken line is used you must not enter the lane if you can avoid it.

Along the edge of the carriageway at a bus stop there is a single yellow line. Such lines indicate waiting or parking restrictions, usually in conjunction with time plates by the roadside.

A single yellow line signifies that waiting is not permitted for at least eight hours between 7am and 7pm on four days of the week or more.

Double yellow lines convey the same message, but with the important addition that there are restricted periods outside these times. A broken yellow line means that 'no waiting' rules are in force for periods other than eight hours between 7am and 7pm. Perhaps a little confusingly, the message is reinforced by yellow lines painted vertically on the kerbs – but these do not refer to waiting on the carriageway or verge except to load or unload, or while passengers board or alight, which is the meaning of the lines on the carriageway itelf. The kerb lines specifically restrict loading and unloading to the periods shown on the accompanying time plates. Two vertical yellow lines mean a restriction is in force on every working day. Three such lines mean that, in addition, there are other times when loading/unloading is banned. A single line shows that there is a restriction that applies for different periods.

Other instances of the use of yellow lines to indicate restrictions on waiting or stopping are the crosshatched boxes restricting entry unless the exit is clear or a right turn is intended, and yellow zigzags joined by a broken yellow line with the words 'School, Keep Clear', indicating that an entrance must be kept clear of stationary vehicles – including those taking children to school or picking them up afterwards.

## Marks on vehicles

Heavy goods vehicles – lorries over 7500kg max. gross weight, trailers over 3500kg gross weight, commercial vehicles or vehicle/trailer combinations longer than 13m, and builders' skips placed in the road are all required to carry rear markings comprising diagonal red/yellow stripes. On lorries and trailers there are horizontal and vertical marks. Skips need carry only vertical markings, one on the left and one on the right. These are 'handed', so that the stripes point upwards towards the centre line. Lorries/trailers are also required to carry 'Long Vehicle' plaques at the rear.

When loads or equipment carried on a vehicle project at front or rear by an overhang exceeding 1.83 metres, an end plate marked in the form of an inverted red triangle hatched with white is mandatory, together with side markers in the form of a horizontal right-angled red triangle with white hatching. In addition, vehicles carrying dangerous goods must display hazard information panels showing the nature of the substances and giving an emergency telephone number.

## Signals to vehicles

A driver is obliged to comply with hand signals given by authorised persons – usually the police or a traffic warden, though under some circumstances firemen, ambulance crews, naval or military personnel and members of other uniformed services may fall into that category.

Only 'Stop' and 'Come on' examples are illustrated in the Highway Code. They fall into categories, of which the first is a signal given to a vehicle approaching from the front. Here, the stop signal is the right arm raised vertically and the hand extended upwards, palm facing the traffic.

The 'come on' signal is also given with the right arm. The hand is turned away from the traffic, and the arm moved to and fro to beckon.

To stop traffic approaching from behind, a constable on point duty would extend his left arm horizontally. To beckon on traffic behind him, he drops his arm so that it is partly extended, and moves it to and fro in the same beckoning action as before.

When he wishes to stop traffic both in front and behind he combines both stop signals – right arm raised vertically, left arm extended horizontally.

When beckoning traffic from the side, he combines the raised right arm to keep approaching traffic halted, while turning his head to wards the traffic at his side and beckoning with the still raised arm.

He may also aid the flow of traffic by beckoning a number of vehicles on, and pointing at the first vehicle he intends to stop.

Similar signals are sometimes given by unauthorised people –

somebody who is guiding a vehicle out of a side entrance, for example. Should you obey such signals or not? Legally, you should not rely on them. In practice, to ignore them might lead to an accident. One possible response is to regard any unauthorised signal as an indication that *something* is about to happen or that *something* ahead of you is amiss. Check your mirrors, and be prepared to slow or stop, being alerted by the signal and then using your own judgement.

## Signals from vehicles

Most signals given from a vehicle consist of lights or horn. Operating an indicator on the right-hand side of your car means that you intend to move out to the right or turn to the right.

Operating the left-hand indicator conveys that you intend to take one of three courses of action – to move in to the left; to turn left; or to stop on the left.

Applying the brakes automatically operates the stoplights. These mean that you are slowing down or stopping.

None of these signals should be used to cover any other situation, but you may well notice that some drivers will keep brake lights illuminated when at a standstill at the end of a traffic queue – especially when visibility is poor – to give extra warning to following traffic. There is no 'official' recognition of such a signal.

Arm signals are used infrequently these days – except for the most important of them, the one that means 'I intend to slow down or stop.' This involves extending the right arm through the open driver's window, and moving it slowly up and down. It *must* be used when you propose to give way to pedestrians at a zebra crossing. It not only helps (with your brake lights) to inform following traffic, but also indicates to the pedestrians (who obviously cannot see your brake lights) that you *are* slowing down and stopping to give way to them.

To signal a right turn manually, simply extend your arm out of the window. To signal a left turn, extend your arm and rotate it anti-clockwise. You'll notice that motorcyclists and cyclists use an extended left arm instead.

When indicating to an authorised person controlling traffic that you wish to turn right, simply use the normal arm signal already described. If, however, you wish to turn left extend your left arm fully, so that it is visible through the screen. Where you wish to go straight ahead, raise your left arm bent upwards from the elbow, palm facing forward.

Headlamp flashing and sounding the horn both have exactly the same meaning – basically, 'I am here.' Both are warnings of approach, and neither should be used for any other purpose – and certainly not as a rebuke or to express annoyance. The driver who never makes mistakes does not exist. Just shake your head sadly, and reflect that sometime or other you too may do something equally silly. Meanwhile, learn from the error that has been made. Be constructive, not aggressive.

Don't try to be mistakenly courteous, either, by flashing your headlamps to show another driver you intend to give way to him. He may well respond and drive happily out of a side turning straight into the path of an oncoming driver who is, correctly, flashing his headlamps as a warning of approach!

# Before You Drive

So much for the theory: now for the practice. The two are, needless to say, complementary. You cannot pass the driving test on theory alone but, equally, without having thoroughly learned the theory you cannot reach the required standards on the road.

## First, the paperwork

The easy way out, of course, is to take the test in a driving school car. There's a lot to recommend it – you will be completely used to handling it; it may well be a newer and more suitable car than your own; the school will have looked after the tax, insurance, and any MOT test, pre-test check or service; and the instructor will be there to act as the necessary accompanying qualified driver on the great day. It's not always easy to find somebody able to take time off work to ride shotgun with you, remember.

With your own car, it's up to you to look after all those odd little details. You must take with you your certificate of insurance and, if applicable, the car's MOT certificate. That's needed for any car from the third anniversary of its first registration onwards.

You must make sure that a valid tax disc is displayed in the legally-required position – the bottom left-hand corner of the windscreen. A valid disc, incidentally, is one that is still within its expiry date. Forget about the '14 days grace' or the home-made 'tax in post' sticker. Legally, a car that is being driven without a current disc displayed – even if it is out of date by only one day, even if you *have* sent off money for renewal – is an unlicensed vehicle that should not even stand on a road, let alone be driven along it. True, the police usually employ their discretion in such matters, but there is still a risk that, if stopped, you could be reported for failure to display a valid tax disc. And the charge would stick.

Not only that, but your insurance applies only if the vehicle is roadworthy *and licensed*. No tax also means that your insurers could repudiate liability should an accident occur.

Perhaps just as bad, from your point of view, is the fact that an examiner who is determined to follow the rules to the letter would be quite justified in refusing to start the test in what, to him, would be plainly an unlicensed vehicle. So, if your tax is due to expire close to your test date, make sure it's renewed early.

You will need to carry your provisional driving licence. Of course, you always do, don't you? But Murphy's Law being what it is, this is just the day when you might leave it in the pocket of your other suit, or in your other handbag. Don't take a chance: assemble all your documents the night before the test, check that they're all there (you *have* remembered your test appointment card, haven't you?) and pick them all up as a bunch before you leave home. As you do so, check just once more to make certain nothing is forgotten.

## A matter of time

But should you leave home at all? Perhaps a glance through the window reveals a sky so dark and lowering that it suggests the end of the world is nigh. There may be rain or sleet. Even snow. You're 99 per cent certain that the test will be cancelled anyway.

Not so. Tests are not washed out by the weather unless there are good operational reasons as well. You won't be asked to undergo assessment in thick fog, for instance, because no worthwhile conclusion could be drawn from a crawl round the test course at walking pace, even if it were safe to do so. No examiner would believe that it was. As a learner, you could hardly be expected to cope with the test on roads that were covered with ice, or with snow obscuring all the road markings. But mere rain – well, that's the luck of the draw.

You don't even know for certain that the bad weather isn't localised, and that the test centre a few miles away isn't basking in sunshine. The answer, of course, is to ring the centre to check whether the test is still on. If there's a cancellation, you'll be given a new, priority booking at no extra charge – but if you don't contact them, and fail to appear in time for your test, you'll have to apply for a new date through 'the usual channels' *and* pay a new fee as well.

One word of warning, though. If you live more than a ten-minute drive from the centre, and your booking is for the first test of the day, you may find that there is not enough time to get through on the phone before the test is due to begin. Test centre phones are not manned on a 24-hour basis. In that case, if you feel that driving there yourself will only result in a nerve-shattered wreck presenting itself for the test, go anyway but ask your supervising driver to take the wheel, while you relax in the passenger seat.

If you do so, however, make sure that your insurance covers another driver – it's a good idea, if you plan to use a regular supervisor, to specify him (or her) as a named driver when you first apply for cover. Yes, your supervisor's own insurance *will* give cover for driving somebody else's vehicle, but only the very minimum required under the Road Traffic Acts to protect third parties. It won't be comprehensive insurance, and it won't cover damage to your vehicle if it ends up wrapped neatly round a lamp post . . .

Whatever the weather, aim to arrive at the test centre with 10-15 minutes in hand. Not longer, because you won't want to be sitting around developing pre-test nerves. Not less, because timings are precise and you may have to find yourself a parking slot when you arrive. You may also decide that you need to find a toilet! Not all test centres run to such public facilities, and you can hardly stop in the middle of your test, so take care of that aspect before you start.

## Check your car

It's not only your personal preparation that needs to be planned. Your car must be fit for the test, too, so reserve time to check it out – preferably the day before it will be needed, or at worst the weekend before.

This isn't mere pedantry, but a vital part of your test. A driving examiner is entitled to abandon the test at any point if he believes the car to be unsafe, or if any part of it has stopped working. He can abandon it almost before it starts if, for example, he notices that the tyres are worn beyond the legal limit, or even that the seat belts are tangled or dirty. You can't blame him. He is being asked to ride in a car driven by a learner of unknown capability. It's his neck that's at risk, and the least he can expect is that the car itself should be roadworthy.

Now, you are not being asked to carry out a major overhaul, merely to ensure that the car is safe and – for its psychological

42

effect, if nothing else – clean.

The first check must be on the most obvious safety item, the tyres. British legal requirements are unexacting: only that there should be a minimum of 1mm of tread over 75 per cent of the tyre face and visible tread on the rest; no cuts or bulges on the sidewalls; and that pressures should be those recommended by the manufacturers.

How do you measure the depth of tread? The only accurate way is to buy a tyre tread depth gauge – an inexpensive but very handy tool – and use it to measure the tread in the centre of the tyre and on the edges. Discard the tyre if there is less than 2mm tread depth – the legal limit of 1mm is not enough to ensure safety.

Buy a good pressure gauge, too, to check the tyre pressures. The gauges on garage air lines lead a hard life, and their readings cannot be relied on. Check pressures only when the tyres are cold – preferably first thing in the morning, before the car turns a wheel. In motion, the tyres warm up, the air inside them expands, and an accurate reading cannot be taken.

Finally, examine each tyre closely and remove any stones embedded in the tread – they could cause a puncture, and if that happens during the test it will have to be abandoned because the examiner's schedule is too tight to allow you the extra ten minutes or so it takes to change a wheel. If you spot any cuts on the sidewalls play safe and have a new tyre. A cut may mean a damaged carcass, which could lead to a blow-out.

Repeat the check for embedded stones just before leaving for the test – just as a precaution.

Now, check and examine all the lamps – indicators included. Make sure they work. Get somebody to operate the brake pedal so you can be sure the brake lights are operating. Ensure that none of the lamps have broken lenses – especially the indicators (including repeaters) and the brake lights. Engage reverse gear to check the reversing lamps too.

Inside the car, check that the warning lights illuminate and extinguish properly, and that all switches are operative.

Test the screen washers and wipers. In use, wiper blades pick up road filth, which is invariably oil, and soon start to smear the screen instead of cleaning it. Lift the arms clear of the screen and apply a cleanser such as Swarfega to the rubbers. Wipe the residue away with a damp cloth, repeating the process until the cloth no longer brings off black deposits. If this fails, renew the rubbers. Screen wiper blades wear with use – the rate is about the same as tyre wear:

about 15,000/20,000 miles per set on average – but at least they're considerably cheaper to replace !

Clean wipers are no use on a filthy screen. Wash all exterior glass thoroughly, using detergent and warm water. Flush with clean water and, preferably, dry off with a chamois leather. Have a damp cloth and the 'chammy' in the car when you go for your test, and on arrival at the test centre give the screens and windows a final clean. Remember that you should arrive there with your screenwasher bottle full, too – and with the jets properly aimed, so that the water hits the screen at eye level each side. Jets that shoot over the car roof clean somebody else's screens, not yours.

You'll need to clean the interior of the screens and windows too. A combination of vapour release from plastic mouldings and dust fed in through heaters and demisters soon puts a film over the inner glass surfaces, reducing visibility. Don't use household cleaner – it causes reflections. Rather buy a special screen-cleaning fluid, or use warm water and detergent, and then a damp cloth dipped in clean water.

During this spring-cleaning session, don't forget that the mirrors, too, will need attention. They must be clean and they must be undamaged. Cracked mirrors are out! Some makers will supply new mirror glasses; others insist on the customer paying for a complete and overpriced mirror. If yours is the latter case, grin and bear it. It's got to be done if you want to pass your test and, more important, you rely on your mirrors for safety. They *must* be up to the job.

Test your car's horn – a mere tap will do – to ensure that it's working; check your handbrake and make sure that it will hold you properly on a gradient – if it won't, either adjust it yourself, or get a garage to do so; and test the main braking system. The pedal should have a firm feel to it, with no more than 1 ½ inches free play before it starts to bite. A 'soft' pedal suggests that air has entered the hydraulic system and that the brakes need to be bled – another job for your garage.

Check that the clutch is properly adjusted, and that there is no 'stiction' in the throttle linkage. A spot of oil on the pivots and any exposed cable works wonders. Set the tickover fast enough to avoid stalling, but not so fast that traffic 'crawls' become tricky.

Under the bonnet, ensure that the sump oil level is correct; that the hydraulic systems are up to their level marks; that the battery is topped up, and that its connections are clean and tight; and that there are spare fuses in the fuse box. If not, buy a spare fuse for

44

each rating required and carry them, wrapped up, in the glove box, together with the owner's manual so you'll know which fuse protects what. If a fuse blows, causing a circuit to fail, you should be allowed enough time to change it, but if you haven't any spares the test will simply be abandoned.

Check the coolant level; and inspect the fan belt for signs of fraying or for maladjustment. If the generator has a separate drive belt, examine that too. Adjust as required.

Apart from ensuring that there is no more than the normal free play at the wheel – just a few degrees of backlash is usual – and that there are no suspicious noises there's nothing much you can do to check the steering.

Lastly, satisfy yourself that the seats are securely fixed and that their adjusters work properly. Check the seat belts, eliminating any twists, and if necessary clean them by wiping with a damp cloth and mild detergent, followed by a wipe with clean water. Make sure that all doors shut securely, and that the windows can be easily lowered and raised.

Remove any mascots that could interfere with your vision – it's better not to have any in the first place, since they can too easily distract your eyes from the road – and finally give the car a thorough clean inside and out. Be particularly careful to ensure that your number plates are clean and easy to read. Then check that your L-plates are securely fitted, and are not so placed that they obstruct vision to either the front or rear. Fill the tank – you don't want to run out of petrol on this of all days – and you are ready for the fray.

Well, almost.


## Please take your seat . . .

The way that you sit has a crucial effect on your ability to drive, and it pays to spend time getting your driving position right.

There is always a temptation to set the driving seat too close to the wheel. This cramps your movements and makes it difficult for you to operate the controls properly.

So start from scratch and see if you can arrive at settings that are right for you. First, push the seat to its rearmost setting, and if it has a seat-rake adjuster use it to bring the back into a position that enables you to hold the wheel comfortably in the 'ten to two' or – better – the 'quarter to nine' position. Your arms should be slightly bent at the elbows, not straight.

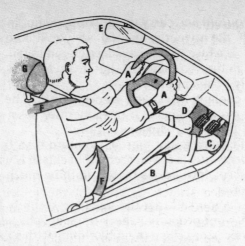

*Points to note when setting up your driving position. A. Grip the wheel at the "quarter to three" position. B. Set the seat so that the pedals are easy to operate, and your arms are slightly bent at the elbows. C. Pivot the throttle foot on its heel and set the pedals so the foot can slide from throttle to brake without lifting. D. Keep the 'idle' left foot clear of the clutch pedal. E. Set the mirror so you need only eye movement to use it. F. Make sure the seat belt is properly adjusted. G. Set the head restraint just clear of the back of your head.*

Too far back? Then move the seat forward one notch, re-adjust the seat-back angle, and try again. Repeat this until you have found the rearmost position that enables you to meet this requirement for steering.

Now, can you reach the pedals without stretching? The accelerator? Usually no problem. The brake? In its static position, perhaps – but can you apply it fully without sliding yourself forward on the seat? If not, move the seat one notch further to the front and try again.

If that's OK, what about the clutch? Here, remember, you don't really need to be able to floor the pedal. A couple of inches movement beyond the point at which the clutch is fully disengaged should be sufficient. Many drivers – experienced, as well as learners, cripple their driving positions simply to gain redundant extra movement on that one pedal.

If you're satisfied with the relationship you've achieved between yourself and the steering wheel and pedals, slip on your seat belt, double-check, and then snick the gear lever into whichever position requires the greatest movement. You should be able to do it without lifting your back away from the seat. If not, bringing the seat-back a little closer to the vertical may do the trick. Otherwise, slide the seat forward one notch and check again.

By trial and error, you should be able to arrive at a driving position that gives you delicate control of the steering and the ability to accelerate, brake and change gear without difficulty or hesitation.

On some cars a little more fine tuning of the settings may be needed to avoid a stretch to some of the less handily placed switches, though here it is permissible to accept a minor amount of movement where they are not controls that are constantly used.

The ability to see out of the car is often dependent more on the height of the seat than on its fore-and-aft location. Some cars – though not enough of them – have built-in height adjustment. In some cases a cushion can be used to raise you, but not if you are long in the back. If you are, you will lose vital lumbar and shoulder support. Any such cushion should be securely strapped down, not placed loose.

Now set your mirrors. Here, you run up against another of those official nonsenses. The ideal mirror setting is one that enables you to make a mirror check just by moving your eyes. In the test, however, that would be classed as only a glance, and deemed 'insufficient'. The examiner will expect you to move your head – though only slightly – whenever you carry out mirror checks as part of a manoeuvre.

You'll just have to humour him – but set your mirrors properly anyway. With the car parked by the kerb, with a clear view behind, first set the interior mirror so that just by switching your gaze to upwards and to the left you obtain a perfect view. You'll find, in practice, that this setting almost makes itself. If you can just see the back of the left side of your head in the right-hand side of the mirror, and the top of the rear screen is just visible in the upper part of the mirror, then the setting should be virtually correct.

Next, note the furthest external object to the right that you can see. Adjust your offside mirror so that this is also just visible in the left of the glass. Select an object far to the left in your interior mirror. Set the nearside door mirror so that it is just visible on the right, and you have the best lateral coverage obtainable with the mirrors fitted to your car.

Vertically, door mirrors should be adjusted to give a reflection from just above your car's waist – judge it by waiting for a car to pass. Track it in your mirrors, passing it from one to the other. If it disappears prematurely from the offside mirror, lowering the glass slightly should ensure that you will arrive at a setting in which you can still see the rear end of an overtaking car just as its bonnet enters your peripheral vision.

It's worth spending time to get these settings exactly right, so that you can appraise situations behind you by rapid eye movements alone.

But remember, during the test you *must* make at least token head movements. Daft, isn't it!

# Starting Up and Moving Off

Driving is an art, not a science, and if you have been keen enough to read a number of books in this, the run-up to your test, you are probably a sorely puzzled learner, for you will have been offered much conflicting advice.

Even the apparently simple operation of turning the steering wheel, you'll conclude, is a subject upon which experts themselves can't agree. On the one hand, the competition driver will be extolling the virtues of crossed-arm steering – 'You can instantly return the front wheels to the straight-ahead position.' Some instructors will recommend a push-pull use of the steering wheel which results in your hands pumping up and down the rim like the pistons of a steam engine. Others, basing their technique upon police driving practice, will have advised a wheel-shuffling technique in which the hands rarely stray more than two or three inches up and down the rim. Some suggest holding the wheel at the '10 to 12' position; others again prefer the 'quarter to three' grip, arguing that it is more comfortable and that it offers maximum use of the available leverage.

Nobody, it seems, is absolutely certain of the right way to use the clutch when moving off. Some suggest bringing up the clutch to biting point, and then holding it there while you check behind, release the hand brake, and then pull away – accompanied, presumably, by a strong smell of scorching friction linings. Others say that the clutch should be held fully out, and release co-ordinated with freeing the handbrake and gently opening the throttle.

Well – a word of warning. For the driving test, *use whatever methods you have been taught*. In your future motoring, you'll have ample time in which to learn which techniques suit you best and your car best. Now is not the time to experiment, still less to start an unlearning process. Providing you move the car away safely and smoothly, drive carefully without wandering around on the road, stop quickly without losing control, and carry out the various manoeuvres effectively, the examiner will not be over-worried about your artistry.

But there are two exceptions. Using the crossed-arms method of steering will guarantee failure – in fact, so will letting either hand stray over the 12 o'clock position, save perhaps during parts of the reversing tests during which you will be steering righthanded and placing your left arm on the back of the front passenger seat to steady yourself.

The other is any attempt to use the 'heel and toe' technique for braking and changing gear at the same time. It's an advanced-driving technique that demands perfect co-ordination, with the car's pedals properly set to make it possible. Used by a learner it could be dangerous. You may have read about it – but now is *not* the time to start practising!

## Before you start

Making the appropriate safety checks before moving off is an integral part of good driving, though the fact that it also forms an essential part of the driving test makes it doubly important. You can fail the test on this point alone.

It begins once the examiner has settled into the front passenger seat and has told you what he now expects you to do: follow the road ahead unless directed otherwise by traffic signs, or on his instructions. He will then invite you to move off when you're ready.

Well, you heard what the man said. Don't sit there waiting for him to tell you to start your engine but, equally, don't just turn the ignition key and bang the car into gear. There's a set sequence of checks that you need to carry out. What's more, you need to make sure that he *knows* you've carried them out, so make the fact quite obvious.

First, you have to ensure that all car doors are firmly shut. So, give a confirming shake on your own door and, in a four-door car, look into the back to visually check the rear doors too. Hatchback drivers should have earned a Brownie point by checking that the tailgate is properly closed as they walked round the back before getting in. It's usual to assume that the examiner will have ensured that his own door is properly closed, out of a sense of self-preservation, if nothing else. However, you should have listened carefully when he entered the car. The satisfying 'clunk' of a properly closed door is quite different from the metallic rattle of one that has only the safety latch engaged. A glance across at it isn't against the rules, but it shouldn't really be necessary.

After the doors, the belts. By now, both you and the examiner should have your belts fastened. Drop your left hand down and check that your buckle is secure and, with an inertia reel belt, also check that the shoulder strap is reeling freely.

Now the seat. Give it a little wiggle fore and aft to double-check that the adjuster mechanism is holding it properly, and then place your hands on the wheel and your feet on the pedals – *not* to check that you can reach them (after all, you have just driven the car to the test centre) but so that the examiner can see that you *have* checked.

Mirrors next. Once again – especially if you've followed the advice given in the previous chapter – your mirrors should already be carefully set. Still, no harm in hamming it up a little, so turn your head slightly to check the view in the interior mirror – hold it momentarily with one finger above the frame and the other below it as if to make a last-minute adjustment, if you want to drive the message home – and then turn your head right and check the offside door mirror; then left to check the nearside.

Now, the handbrake. Of course it's on – you applied it before leaving the car on arrival. But check all the same: just drop a hand to it and (without touching the button) give a token upward caress just to make sure.

Lastly, move your hand forward on the gear level and waggle it from side to side, showing that it is in neutral.

From now on – if you haven't already formed the habit – carry out this same cockpit check every time you enter your car. It will avoid, at best, danger – at least, embarrassment – come the day when you leave the car parked in gear on a slope and quite forget until you turn the ignition key . . .

Start the engine. You can give it a touch of throttle if need be, but don't let it race and don't blip the throttle, especially if your car has a sportier-than-usual exhaust note. You are not on the grid at Brands Hatch.

With the engine idling reliably, you are ready to move away: but not before you have carried out an all-round visual check that you can do so without endangering or inconveniencing any other road users – drivers, motorcyclists, cyclists, equestrians, pedestrians.

Use your judgement here. There's no need to stay riveted to the spot simply because you can see an old lady on a bicycle labouring slowly towards you 400 yards away. That would doubtless be classed as 'undue hesitation.' The acid test is whether you can move out and accelerate to cruising speed without causing other road users to slow or take evasive action.

If your use of the mirrors suggests that it's safe to move off, engage first gear, keep the clutch depressed, look quickly over your right shoulder to check your blind spot, signal a right turn, look ahead, and in one coordinated movement bring the clutch to biting point and give a little more throttle as you release the handbrake. By now, both hands should be on the wheel, ready to steer the car in whichever direction is appropriate – something that depends, of course on your starting position.

Once the car is moving, let the clutch fully home and increase speed as required by giving more throttle.

Circumstances – and your car – will dictate when to make the first gear-change. Some cars have wide-ratio gearboxes in which first is very low, demanding an early change to avoid over-revving. The only sure guide is to follow the routine in which you have been instructed, which will have taken that factor into account. Meantime, as soon as your pulling away manoeuvre is completed, check that your indicator has cancelled – some will only do so if there has been a pronounced counter-turn of the wheel. If it's still operating, cancel it manually.

Your car should now be ready for the change into second gear, and the drill for that and subsequent changes is always the same. Throttle closed and clutch out in one co-ordinated movement. As the clutch disengages, move the gear lever and then quickly let the clutch home again. Don't slip it. Equally, don't just take your foot off the pedal and let it home with a bang. The examiner doesn't like jerky driving. As the clutch re-engages, gently open the throttle. And, while you're doing all that, keep your eyes on the road: don't glance down at the lever or the pedals.

## Pulling away from a parking place

At some point in the test you will be asked to pull into a restricted parking place behind another vehicle, and then pull away again.

Make things easy for yourself, when pulling up, by coming to rest at least half a car's length behind the vehicle in front. A car's length

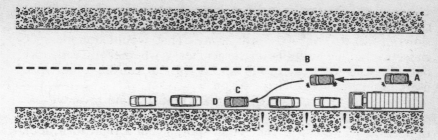

*Sequence for parking in a restricted space. A. Position the car left of the centre line, nearside clearance permitting; check mirrors, signal left, slow down. B. Turn towards kerb; leave 1m clearance from parked vehicles; left indicator still on. C. Straighten up to stop 12-18 inches from kerb; handbrake on; neutral; check indicators off. D. Allow between half car-length and a full car-length clearance for moving off. Danger points = !*

is even better – no more, or somebody in a Fiat 126 will almost certainly nip in ahead of you! Giving yourself space means that you will be able to get away again without reversing.

Follow the normal routine – 'mirrors - signal - manoeuvre' – when pulling in, and look particularly for two-wheelers that may be trying to squeeze through on your left. Once you're sure the road is clear, signal left, reduce speed, engage one of the lower gears, and steer carefully to come to rest with your nearside wheels no more than a foot from the kerb. If you *have* to make a mistake here be a few inches further out rather than hit the kerb, but accuracy is really all-important in this part of the test.

So remember what you have been taught – that from your normal sitting position the apparent kerb line will cut through your bonnet at one particular point when your clearance is correct. Get that intersection spot on, draw up parallel to the kerb, apply the handbrake, and then – but only then – select neutral.

Fine. Now all you have to do is pull out again. Wait for the examiner to tell you to move off when you are ready, and again go through the 'mirrors - signal - manoeuvre' routine. If your mirror check reveals other traffic aproaching from the rear, it's better to let it pass before continuing – this is a slow manoeuvre. Check again in your mirrors, and when you judge you have ample time to pull away indicate a right turn. Engage first gear, give a look over your shoulder to check the blind spot, then release the handbrake and move away slowly, steering to the right as you do so. Turn the wheel as you begin to move, but not before. Turning the wheel on a

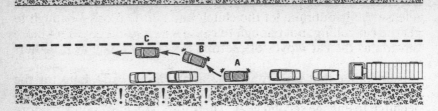

*Sequence for pulling away from a restricted parking space. A. Check mirrors, and visual observation all round; signal right; engage first gear; release handbrake and pull away. B. If unsighted, move only far enough to allow assessment of traffic, then wait until clear; right indicator still on; continue when safe. C. Straighten up; check indicators off; drive on; reposition car 1m from kerb when possible. Watch for dangers – particularly emerging pedestrians or vehicles pulling out, where marked by "!"*

stationary car is marked as a steering fault.

Where your rear vision is badly restricted, it is usually permissible to ease slowly out just enough to enable you to make a second check, though this should be avoided whenever possible. Why make two starts instead of one? Either way, keep checking the road behind *and in front* (a pedestrian might step out from the other end of that lorry behind which you parked!) as you engage the clutch and drive away.

Straighten up, accelerate to the appropriate speed (again, check that your indicators have cancelled: if not, cancel them manually) and resume your drive.

## Hill starts

Restarting on a gradient demands good coordination of throttle, clutch and handbrake, for the obvious reason that without it you will roll backwards and probably fail the test.

The actual pull-away will be simple enough, for the examiner will be careful not to ask you to carry out this manoeuvre where the way ahead is obstructed. So the normal routine for pulling away from the kerb applies – 'mirrors – signal – manoeuvre.'

As always, check carefully for cyclists. Make sure, too, that there are no pedestrians about to cross the road immediately behind your car – if there are, and you roll back, the resulting accident could be fatal. Signal a right turn, and when you are sure all is clear, bring the clutch to biting point and apply higher-than-usual revs. As you release the handbrake let the clutch bite a little more – enough to get the car rolling, not enough to cause a jerk – and give a bit more throttle as the car moves off, letting the clutch home as it gathers way.

Remember that gravity will be applying an extra load for the engine to overcome, and that it will decelerate the car when you declutch to engage second gear. Therefore, you must build up more momentum than usual in first gear before changing, and be sure not to fumble selection of second. It must go home first time – and quickly. Watch it! If you try to 'snatch' the change you may miss it altogether. A firm and accurate hand on the gearlever is essential.

Lastly check that the indicator has cancelled, and then engage higher gears according to the demands of the terrain.


## Downhill start

The approved method of making a downhill start – a manoeuvre that is sometimes tested, though not as commonly as uphill starts – is to use the footbrake to hold the car during take-up of the clutch.

The pull-away itself is standard practice – all the normal safety checks and signals are required – but the technique differs from that for an uphill start in its later stages.

To move away, engage first gear (second is permissible if the gradient is steep) and, with the clutch depressed, fully apply the footbrake. Keeping both pedals depressed, let off the handbrake and release the clutch pedal to biting point. Then slowly release the footbrake. As the car begins to move, let the clutch fully home and transfer your right foot on to the accelerator. How much throttle is needed depends upon the steepness of the hill – a factor that also governs the gear that is appropriate. A steep gradient may require second gear to remain engaged: otherwise, third gear is the highest likely to be needed.

# Stop!

Let's start by taking a bit of simplified theory on braking into account. A brake, of course, works by friction. When you press the pedal, you bring its linings – which are fixed to the car – into contact with the brake disc or drum that rotates with each wheel. The friction between the two surfaces absorbs the energy that is driving the car forward and converts it into heat, which is then dissipated into the mass of the brakes and subsequently into the air. As the energy is absorbed, the car slows, and finally stops.

Think about that for a moment, and you'll realise that this process can only take place if there is relative movement between the brake disc/drum and its linings. No movement, no friction. No friction, no energy absorption. A 'locked' brake is a brake that is not working!

But, the car still stops. The task of absorbing energy is transferred to the 'footprints' – the four modestly-sized contact areas between the tyres and the road surface. The car simply skids, relying on the friction between the tyre face and the ground to absorb its energy. Since the tyre is far less efficient as a heat converter, skidding to a halt involves an increase in the stopping distance. Worse, while the front wheels are locked the car cannot be steered – the wheels *must* be rotating for steering control to be retained. You are not just making a less effective stop, but are out of control as well!

It follows that the way in which one can brake most efficiently is to apply the footbrake to the point at which the wheels are still turning, but only just. Unfortunately, that's easier to say than to do, unless you have a car fitted with an anti-lock braking system that performs the job for you.

Nor is it easy for a learner who is faced with the need for a sudden stop – either in a genuine emergency, or in the simulation of one in the driving test – to avoid the natural instinct to slam the brakes on. Even experienced drivers can tend to turn 'panic stops' into just that by over-application of the brakes.

Ideally, when you need to stop quickly you should apply a constant firm pressure to the brake pedal, holding it just short of the point at which the wheels would lock. Several factors militate against this, but some at least are within your control.

For a start, the pedal layout on many cars is not ideal. In the 0.7 seconds of your reaction time, you need to release the accelerator and transfer your foot on to the brake. Sounds simple – but just give a thought to the mechanics of the operation. To release the throttle, you probably have to lift your foot – so it is already going the wrong way. The temptation is then to move it sideways, heel brushing the floor, and stamp it down on to the pedal – a leg movement. The almost inevitable result is to use up valuable time. If you lose only a tenth of a second, that represents an extra four feet covered at 30mph before braking has even begun.

It's far better if you can make the entire operation little more than an ankle movement. Keep your heel on the floor, release the accelerator by bending your foot upwards at the ankle joint – using the heel as a fulcrum – and then pivot it to the left about the heel, straight on to the brake pedal. You are then in a position to apply a controlled, firm pressure. Or, rather, you would be had your pedals been so set that you could do it. All to often you are likely to find that, far from falling squarely on the pad of the brake pedal, the sole of your shoe strikes the side of it instead.

All is not lost! Most braking systems incorporate some means of adjusting pedal height. Sometimes it's done by screwing the yoke on the operating pushrod in or out; sometimes by means of an adjustable stop; sometimes by varying the position of a stoplamp switch. The range of adjustment is unlikely to be large – perhaps a couple of millimetres – but it could make all the difference.

If the correct relationship between the pedals cannot be obtained by that adjustment alone, there's another shot in the locker. The accelerator pedal arm is often made from steel rod, and this can be bent, cold, to raise or lower the pad.

Don't try to carry out these modifications yourself. Go to an approved agent, explain what's needed, and have the job done professionally. It should be quick, and reasonably inexpensive.

If, after that, you're still having trouble making a quick switch from accelerator to brake, try changing your shoes. Stout walking shoes may have a sole up to 10mm thick. Buy a special pair of driving shoes that can be slipped on whenever you get into the car. These will have thin soles – better for obtaining the 'feel' of the pedals – that are less likely to catch the edges of the pads. As a bonus, they usually have rounded heels, too, making your 'pivot point' more efficient.

After all these aids have been applied, you should certainly find quick and delicate brake control easier, but the right touch can only come with constant practice. Obviously you can't spend hours driving up and down a road constantly braking and accelerating, but do ask your instructor to give you as much practical experience on this point as possible. If you are using your own car, and you know of a large car park that can be guaranteed to be quiet early in the morning, it might be possible to use its wide open spaces for a few minutes each day. If so, don't choose one close to houses – you could be cautioned by the police for causing a nuisance.

There's no risk of that if, instead, you sit quietly in your car, in your own driveway or garage, or at the roadside, just practising the 'accelerator to brake' movement over and over again, accustoming your mind and your muscles to the action. With the engine off you won't obtain the 'feel' of the brake pedal – but you can't do that at a standstill anyway.

## Tyres and surfaces

No matter how good your brakes or how adroit you are in applying them, there are two other vital factors in safe stopping. One is the grip offered by your tyres; the other the state of the road surface.

First, the tyres. If they are to do their job, they must have adequate tread and they must be set at the correct pressures.

Oddly enough, in dry conditions a tyre that is worn down to the legal limit offers better grip than a new one. Where a brand-new tyre, with 7mm or so of tread, gives a coefficient of friction at 30mph of about 0.85, the worn tyre puts more rubber on the road and returns a coefficient of 1.0. Fine! If you intend to do all your driving in the arid heat of Death Valley, just carry on using a worn tyre – it's the closest you'll come to the racing slicks fitted to Grand Prix cars.

In Britain, though, rumour has it that occasional rain can be expected and the roads then get wet. With only surface dampness – a depth of water of just 0.2mm (eight thousandths of an inch) the new tyre's coefficient of friction drops to 0.65, but the worn tyre's plummets to 0.5.

Heavy rain is defined as a surface water depth of 1mm (40 thousandths of an inch). The new tyre's coefficient falls to 0.55, the worn tyre's to 0.44. And in puddles (that's water 2 mm deep, about a sixteenth of an inch) while the new tyre retains a respectable coefficient of 0.5 the worn tyre is down to 0.25 and you're in big trouble! Put the speeds up to 55 mph and in heavy rain the old tyre will give about as much grip as a new tyre offers on ice. The reason is simple: the new tyre has channels (tread) to force the water away from the vital contact patch, and little cross-cuts (sipes) on the contact patch itself to squeegee the contact area dry. You'll have seen the result on any damp road – the traffic 'line' is marked by dry areas where passing tyres have cleared away the water. Beyond it, the road surface is still wet. If your tyres are worn, *even to the legal limit*, you cannot brake properly.

Tyre pressures are also important. The pressures specified by the makers are those that will give the best 'footprint' in contact with the road. Pressures that are too low or too high distort this vital contact patch, and reduce grip. Low pressures are particularly deadly, since they also allow excessive flexing of the sidewalls, making steering less accurate and tyre failure more likely.

Road surfaces, too, have varying degrees of skid-proofing. The first rain after a prolonged dry spell – especially light rain – forms a slippery emulsion of tyre rubber, oil and road dirt. In autumn, wet leaves on the surface offer little more grip than ice. From the start of your driving, learn to watch road surfaces carefully and plan accordingly.

The last factor in the equation is speed. The faster you go, the longer it takes you to stop – and speed is a factor fully within your control. Learn by heart the braking distances given in the Highway Code – they are based on good practice, using the police formula that the stopping distance in feet of a car on a good dry tarmac surface is given by squaring the speed in miles per hour and dividing by 20. Accept this as gospel, and don't be misled by press road tests that may give much more favourable braking distances for your car. The conditions are entirely different. The road test car was being driven at a steady speed by a skilled and experienced tester who knew precisely the point at which he intended to brake, and was prepared to do so. It is not a result you could expect to reproduce in an emergency.

Throughout the driving test your aim will be to slow in good time and pull up gently, except in the emergency stop exercise, which is designed to test your competence in taking immediate and effective action – your reaction, in other words.

The normal procedure is that the examiner will tell you that, very shortly, he will ask you to stop 'as in an emergency'. The signal he will give you is that, as he says 'Stop' he will also tap the dashboard or the windscreen, usually with his test board. It's up to you to stop, under control, as quickly as you can once the signal has been given.

This is the one occasion in the test when you do *not* follow the 'mirrors-signal-manoeuvre' routine. Before he gives you his signal the examiner himself will have checked the road situation behind with a careful look over his right shoulder, and he won't ask you to stop if there could be any danger to (or from) following traffic. Spot his backward glance, and you have a split-second more to prepare yourself. Don't initiate the stop at that point, though. You *must* await his signal. When you get it, simultaneously release the accelerator and slide your foot across to the brake pedal – easy, if you've followed the advice given earlier in this chapter. Apply firm pressure, trying to judge pedal movement so that the brakes are on the point of locking. Hold the pedal still then, as the car slows towards a standstill, gradually release the pressure. Remember, too, that you should check in your mirrors *after* you have started to brake.

During braking, hold the car in a straight line and be alert for the first signs of the wheels locking up. Sometimes you can feel a slight bump as lock-up commences, though for most drivers the first intimation is the screech of tyres on the road. If you can anticipate that, so much the better. Feel the bump, and immediately ease the pedal slightly so that the wheels can turn again. If a skid has actually started, ease the pedal rather more – *don't* release it completely – and then re-apply pressure to just before lock-up point.

Be particularly careful to keep the wheels straight if the car skids. There will be no apparent effect if you turn the steering with the wheels locked, but as soon as you release the brake pedal and the wheels start to rotate the car will immediately swerve whichever way the wheels are pointing, and you could have an emergency all of your own making on your hands.

There is one more control involved in this part of the emergency stop – the clutch. Your instinct will tell you that as you brake you should free the clutch – and your instinct will be right in some instances. Not this one, though. Keep the clutch engaged until the car has slowed perceptibly, then depress it and keep it down until you come to a standstill. With the clutch home, and the wheels still turning, you get a little extra braking effect as the engine over-runs, and you avoid what is essentially a panic reaction. Don't leave clutch disengagement too long, though, or you'll stall the engine.

With the car safely at a standstill, and the clutch and brake pedals still depressed, apply the handbrake. Then, and only then, move the gearlever into neutral.

Pull away again when asked – and don't, in the excitement of the moment, now forget to carry out your normal 'mirrors – signal – manoeuvre' routine.

## Emergency use of the handbrake

The handbrake has a dual purpose. Its primary function is as a parking brake, but it is also a separate emergency braking system.

Since virtually every car built today has a split hydraulic brake circuit to ensure that at least one pair of brakes will continue to operate after a systems failure, this 'belt and braces' aspect of the handbrake is usually overlooked and it does not form part of the driving test.

However, you do need to know about it, since you might experience a main brake failure in the course of the test, and primarily you are the driver so it's up to you to deal with it.

The first action is to get into as low a gear as possible as quickly as possible. Third should be easy to engage, but second gear is preferable. This gives reasonable engine braking with the accelerator pedal released, and it's a viable move if the road is clear.

If there's a hazard ahead, though, the handbrake has to be your first resort. Leave the clutch engaged, release the accelerator, and drop your left hand on to the brake lever. Depress the button, and apply the lever. Don't release the button – just 'play' the pressure applied to the lever so that the rear wheels (on which most handbrakes operate) don't lock and skid. Release the clutch just when the car is on the point of stopping, and fully apply the handbrake to hold it.

# Go Ahead

A fair slice of the driving test consists of basically following the road ahead – a welcome change, you may think, from the set-piece manoeuvres. This is where you can relax a bit and just enjoy the drive. And you couldn't be more wrong!

Each test route (and every test centre has a choice of circuits available) has been carefully selected to produce a miscellany of driving environments, each of equal difficulty. The examiner will be watching the way you cope with them. He will be expecting you – to use the jargon – to 'make progress by driving at a speed appropriate to the road and traffic conditions', neither speeding nor dawdling. He will want to be convinced that you are making proper use of your controls; using your mirrors; giving the right signals in good time; taking prompt and appropriate action to comply with road signs, road markings, traffic lights, and signals from road controllers and other vehicles.

It's on this part of the test, too, that he can assess if you overtake safely; observe the correct procedures when meeting or crossing the paths of other vehicles; take the right action at pedestrian crossings; show awareness of the actions of others, and anticipate them as you should. He'll expect to see adequate clearances allowed when driving past stationary vehicles and proper care in the use of speed.

In short, this is the part of the test that will help most to convince him that you have not only studied the Highway Code, but that you are able to put it into practice.

It will usually follow the drawing up and pulling away exercises, and possibly the emergency stop too. Assuming that you have started off after parking in a restricted space, you will now be driving smoothly and straight, your car positioned at least 3ft (1 m) from the kerb. Your speed will be appropriate to the conditions, and you will be in the correct gear.

What's the appropriate speed? That's for you to judge. If the road is one subject to a 30mph limit, then just under 30mph would be about right, assuming that the road ahead is clear of hazards. If there is heavy traffic, light-controlled junctions, pedestrian crossings – anything that might present you with a dangerous situation – then your speed must be reduced accordingly. In a crowded shopping centre even 20mph or less may be the right speed.

And the right gear? Again, it depends entirely on the car you are driving – another good reason for using the vehicle on which you have trained. In town conditions, fifth gear on a five-speeder is usually too high, so fourth (or even third) would be better. On a four-speeder, third normally gives you better control, with a bit of engine in hand for emergencies. But try at some point in the test – perhaps where the route includes a stretch of clear 40mph limited road – to use the highest gears just enough to show the examiner that you know they exist, providing their use appears *to you* to be appropriate for the conditions.

Hold a steady course on the wheel. Don't over-control – a little movement goes a long way providing you give your car a fraction of a second to settle. Turn the wheel too much, too quickly, and you'll simply initiate a frantic dart at the kerb or the centre-line, which then has to be corrected. On a steadily-moving car, little more than firm pressure on the wheel is required to keep it straight, and only an inch or so of wheel movement to set it up for gentle curves. Remember, too, that if there is any significant camber on the road the car's natural tendency will be to run down it. You can balance it nicely for straight-line driving simply by applying enough pressure to hold the wheels against the camber.

Avoid *excessive* use of the mirrors. Most of your attention needs to be focused where you're going, not where you've been. Make frequent quick mirror checks to keep yourself up to date with traffic conditions behind you, so you can plan your driving, but don't stare into them. Even at 30mph your car is travelling at 44 feet per second, so if you spend just one second contemplating the view behind you there may be a nasty shock awaiting when you look to the front again! Add on the 30 feet thinking distance required at 30mph, and you might have an accident just waiting to happen 70-odd feet ahead before you can even apply your brakes.

Now let's follow through on a typical urban drive, meeting those everyday situations with which you will have to cope.

The first is a matter of positioning. You are on a normal two-lane carriageway, and ahead of you is a line of cars parked by the kerb. Are you in the right position on the road to pass them? No, you're not – you were cruising just a metre out from the kerb, remember. Therefore, you need to change position. What do you do?

First, initiate your action sequence – 'mirrors-signal-manoeuvre.' Is there following traffic about to overtake you? If so, you must hold your course and slow down – an action which makes the other vehicle's overtaking manoeuvre shorter by increasing its relative speed, and also gives you a little more time in which to carry out your subsequent manoeuvre too.

Your mirror check shows that its safe for you to pull out. You are already in the appropriate gear, so you signal with your offside indicators, and move over to your new position on the road, in good time to pass the stationary vehicles safely.

But are you safe? Or, rather, are other road users safe? How much clearance are you leaving to your left? A couple of feet? That's not enough!

Consider. Any one of those vehicles could contain a driver who wishes to get out to do some shopping. There's no guarantee that he'll take the precaution of checking for oncoming traffic before flinging his offside door wide open. You must allow for that possibility. So what types of vehicle are parked there? Lorries? Then expect a door three feet wide to appear suddenly in the *upper* part of your sightline – they're high vehicles, as well as long ones.

A three-door hatchback, perhaps? Like sports cars, these have very wide doors – typically, four feet, compared with the three-foot doors fitted to four-door saloons and estates. If you pass within four feet of it, and it is flung open, there will either be an accident, or a very near miss. A clearance of five feet (1.5 m) should be adequate to guard against any carelessly-opened door, so you adopt that as your position on the road, make sure your indicator has cancelled, check your speed (20 to 25mph should be about right for this only moderately busy road) and look ahead.

Now, what other hazards might you encounter. Right! The most vulnerable and fallible of them all – pedestrians. That line of vehicles (six of them, say) provides six points at which a pedestrian might step out in front of you without warning. That can be anticipated – so look carefully as you approach. A shadow cast on the road between two of the parked cars. A pair of feet glanced in the gap underneath one. It may simply be the driver returning, and waiting for you to pass so that he can walk round the rear of his car and open his door. But it may be a harassed shopper, whose mind is on other things, who may simply start to cross the road without looking. Weigh up the possibilities, watch for signs of sudden movement, and decide whether this may be an appropriate moment to give a short warning toot on the horn as a precaution. And mentally prepare yourself to make an emergency stop – this time for real – if the shadow proves to be a child intent on reaching that sweet shop on the other side of the road. An impulsive child has a deadly rate of initial acceleration . . .

The obstacle passed, you now return to your original road position unless doing so would involve you pulling out again within a short distance to avoid yet more parked vehicles. Don't weave around such obstructions as if you were on an obstacle course – simply keep straight on until you can settle back on your line 1m from the kerb for a reasonable distance. When you return to it, carry out the full routine ('mirrors - signal - manoeuvre': you must know that by heart by now!) and don't be tempted to swerve sharply back towards the kerb. Move in at a gentle angle, so that there are no hurried control movements to make. The examiner wants a smooth ride, remember.

Now the road ahead is straight and clear, with no side turnings visible, no traffic signs except, about a quarter of a mile ahead, what is obviously the start of a 40mph speed limit. You judge that if you start accelerating now, you will just be up to a nice, steady 40mph by the time you reach the signs. So you do – and you have just failed your test! Why? Because you have exceeded the speed limit. The 40mph limit begins at the signs, and not even a fraction of an inch before. You could and should increase your speed to 30mph (a speed appropriate to the conditions) and you should certainly not maintain 30mph after passing the signs, because you could be impeding following traffic.

So check your mirrors and if there is nobody close behind and obviously about to overtake speed up to an indicated 30mph. Or, rather, be on the safe side and keep the needle just on the slow side of 30. The examiner will be checking your speed constantly, but from where he's sitting his view will be distorted by parallax. A needle dead on the 30mph mark will appear to him to be about 2mph past it. He's experienced, and he may make allowance for it. Again, he may not: but as he is most unlikely to mark you down for being 2mph *under* a limit set the needle at around 28mph for 30mph zones and 38mph where the maximum is 40 – assuming, of course, that it is safe to do so.

A few hundred yards further on, a '30' sign appears. That means you must be down to no more than 30mph by the time you reach it – don't bowl merrily into the lower-limited area in the blithe assurance that you're entitled to do 40mph until you pass the sign. It marks the *start* of the new limit, not the *end* of the old one. So, in good time, check your mirrors, lose speed slowly with a gentle touch on the brakes – enough to kill the excess 10mph and to bring on your stoplamps to signal to following traffic that you are slowing – and resume your near-30mph cruise, still keeping your safe distance from the kerb.

You now encounter a moving hazard – a milk float, making heavy weather of its 15 mph cruise. You need to overtake.

First, check that the road ahead is clear for a distance sufficient for you to complete the manoeuvre safely, without endangering or inconveniencing other road users. They include the milk float and its driver. During your look ahead, make sure there are no side turnings to the right from which other traffic might emerge, or into which the milk float itself may wish to turn. The driver may, after all, still be making his rounds.

When you are satisfied that it's all clear ahead, apply the routine. Your mirror check should convince you that nothing else is close enough to be preparing to overtake you, so you can prepare to pass the milk float. You'll have closed on him by now – but not by too much. Your speed is approaching 30mph, so applying the separation rule laid down in the Highway Code (1m for each mile per hour of speed) you should maintain a minimum separation of 30m (98ft). That's a good six car lengths. If you can avoid getting closer to it than that, there is no reason why you should not maintain your present speed when overtaking. Another check ahead; another mirror check, then signal, and move to the right into a position that will allow you to pass with ample clearance – again, at least one metre. You may straddle the centre-line if necessary, *unless* it is a double white line with the solid line nearest you. But then, you would have observed that during your initial appreciation, wouldn't you?

After passing, check in your mirror, and signal that you are returning to your original position 1m out from the kerb. Don't cut in sharply – particularly as the car will now be travelling down the camber. Come in at an angle of about 30 degrees, slanting smoothly back to your course, and straighten up gently.

Signs warn you that you are approaching a roundabout, at which the examiner has asked you to take the road leading off to the

66

right. You need, therefore, to position yourself just to the left of the centre-line on the approach. As always, begin by checking the road behind you in your mirrors. If you are sure it is safe to do so, signal your intention by operating your offside indicators – then check again in the mirrors, and look ahead to make sure that your manoeuvre would not endanger or inconvenience oncoming traffic either. If you are satisfied on both counts, pull out to the right and take up position. You need to leave the left-hand side of the road clear for traffic turning left or going straight ahead at the roundabout.

Now reduce speed (after another mirror check, of course), braking gently so that your stoplamps indicate that you are slowing. As your speed drops, select the right gear for the junction. That will depend upon circumstances – perhaps second gear if observation across the roundabout shows your exit route to be clear and there is no traffic approaching it from the right; first gear if you believe you may have to give way.

Check that your right-hand indicator is still signalling a right-hand turn, and approach the junction. Don't cross the 'Give way' road marking if there is traffic from the right on the roundabout. Wait until the road is clear, then take the right-hand lane around the roundabout, maintaining a constant distance from the offside kerb. Keep indicating a right turn until you are passing the exit before the one that you intend to take, which is the point at which you change your indication to a left-hand turn. Before you reach it, however, glance left to ensure that no traffic is likely to attempt to enter the roundabout before you clear it. Then switch on your left-hand indicator, and turn left into your exit. If possible, take up your correct position 1m from the left-hand kerb as you make progress down the new road. If there are obstructions, however, keep in the right-hand lane until it is safe to change lanes, applying the normal routine.

No time to relax! About 200 yards ahead there is a junction controlled by traffic lights. Green is showing. That should warn you that, by the time you reach them, they will either have changed or be about to change, so be prepared to slow and stop if necessary. The examiner has made no request for you to turn at the junction, so your intended direction is straight ahead. You can see there are two lanes, and mentally select the lefthand one that will allow you to maintain your present position.

Anticipating that a stop will probably be necessary, you check your mirrors, and as you look ahead again the amber light shows.

You have already adjusted your speed as a result of anticipation, and your car has an appropriate gear engaged, so you brake gently and, as the car comes almost to a standstill, you declutch, engage neutral, and apply the handbrake. Now, just short of the stop line, you wait for the lights to change.

Another learner approaching from your left just beats the amber, attempts to turn left in too high a gear, and suddenly stops, blocking the lefthand lane of the road straight ahead. The engine has stalled. At the same moment, the lights turn to green. Do you move into the junction, or not?

No, you don't. The Highway Code is emphatic on the point – 'Do not go forward when the traffic lights are green unless there is room for you to clear the junction safely' – so you remain where you are and ignore the indignant hooting of cars behind you waiting to turn left. You should only move off (and then only to the left) if the examiner specifically asks you to do so.

By the time the lights have completed another cycle, the learner driver has contrived to restart his engine and the way ahead is clear. You will have engaged first gear, ready to move off, as the red and amber lights came up, but you do not release the handbrake and start to let in the clutch until you have a green light and you have checked that the road ahead is clear, with no pedestrian making a last-minute dash across your side of the carriageway from the centre island. As you move, look to the right to make sure that nobody is gambling his life (and yours) by jumping the red lights, and do the same to the left. Resume your drive, positioning yourself a metre from the kerb, in the appropriate gear and at the appropriate speed.

Your next instruction from the examiner is to turn right at the next junction. Even from a distance, you can see that it is marked by an inverted triangle sign and that there is a solid white line on the road. You don't need to wait until you can read the plate on the sign: these two clues alone tell you that you are required to stop at the junction, not just give way, and you already know that you have to turn right. You therefore apply the now-familiar routine and, when you are certain it is safe to do so, move over so that your offside wheels are just to the left of the centre-line, and draw up a little short of the Stop line. Leave your right-hand indicator on.

The road that you are joining is a dual carriageway, but one subject to a 40mph speed limit. The gap in the central reservation facing you is wide enough for you to be able to wait there if necessary. You keep checking traffic approaching from your right,

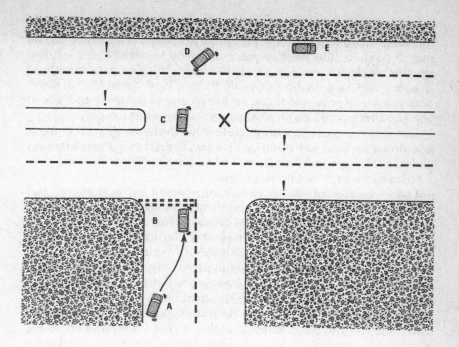

*Sequence for turning right on to a dual carriageway. A. Position the car 1m from the kerb; check mirrors, signal a right turn, move to just left of the centre-line; brake. B. Stop. Observation to right, left, right; give way to traffic on major road; assess if gap in central reservation is wide enough to allow you to halt there – if not, wait until all carriageways are clear; right indicator still on. C. When safe, move forward into centre gap; halt if necessary; when clear, continue; right indicator still on. Unless road markings indicate otherwise, do not move into the area 'X' of centre reservation gap. D. Start right turn before reaching centre line. E. Straighten up and continue to drive 1m from the kerb. Check right indicator cancelled. Look for dangers, including fast-moving traffic that may possibly be overtaking, where marked "!"*

and wait for a suitable gap in the flow to enable you to move off safely. As the last cars in the gaggle approach the junction you check in your mirrors that all is safe behind, engage first gear, and prepare to release the handbrake and move into the gap in the central reservation. The last two cars approaching from your right go by, but a car in the right-hand lane of the other carriageway is approaching the gap, slowing, and signalling a right-hand turn.

Do you move forward into the gap, or not? There are no road markings there to guide turning traffic, and there is a danger that he may turn short into the gap, expecting you to come to his left and pass nearside to nearside. You, however, wish to pass offside to offside, to obtain the best possible field of view down the carriageway you are to join, and if you now drive out to the left-hand side of the gap there could be confusion and consequent danger.

But will the examiner appreciate your motives, or will he mark you down for 'undue hesitancy.' He has been sitting there virtually silent – 'like a robot,' as your instructor may have warned you. Explanations may not be welcome.

One way around that is to talk to yourself for a moment. Just remark, to nobody in particular, 'Hmm. I'm not sure of this chap's intention. He may turn short and create a danger. I'll wait just a few seconds until his intentions are clear.' The examiner can't really avoid overhearing your conversation with yourself, can he?

Your fears were justified. The approaching car turns short into the gap, makes an untidy exit, and passes down the adjoining lane of your carriageway after a dog-leg turn. Not a very good example to a learner – but the road is now clear (you check behind and to each side) so you move straight over into the left-hand side of the gap, pause to recheck that you can rejoin the dual carriageway without danger, and check that nobody has followed you in and is waiting to your right, in your blind spot. If all is clear, turn smoothly across the road to join the left-hand lane, take up your appropriate position, and set up your cruise at an indicated 38 mph.

Ahead, a road sign – a red-bordered triangle bearing a symbol that reminds you of a tuning fork – warns you that the dual carriageway is about to end. As a matter of course, you check in your mirrors and find that a few yards behind, in the outer lane, a car is shaping up to pass. Road space is running short before the carriageways converge, and you have a choice of accelerating to keep ahead of him, slowing to let him by, or holding your speed and risking a close encounter in a bottleneck.

What do you do? You follow the Code's advice and slow down. As the dual carriageway ends, a 30mph limit begins, and a few hundred yards further on you can see a zebra crossing being used by pedestrians. It has a refuge in the middle.

When you are about 50 yards away, the road ahead of you is clear of pedestrians, but some are crossing from the other side towards the refuge. One old lady reaches it first, puts a tentative foot on the crossing, sees you coming, withdraws it, places it back on the crossing. She is obviously dithering about whether to leave the safety of the island or not.

Your course of action is clear. Quickly, you wind down your window, check in the mirror that there is proper clearance between your car and following traffic, release the accelerator, brake gently, and extend your arm, moving it up and down to signal that you are slowing and propose to stop. Then quickly replace your right hand on the wheel, and stop. Apply your handbrake and engage neutral. As the pedestrians cross, wind up your window and maintain a mirror check. When your side of the crossing is clear, you are free to proceed – a normal moving-away operation.

You have now encountered a fair selection of driving hazards and have, hopefully, made only minor errors during this part of the test – if any.

But some more set-pieces remain before you get that coveted pass certificate . . .

# In Reverse

With the possible exception of the emergency stop, the manoeuvres that include reversing are perhaps the part of the test that candidates fear most. It isn't easy, even for experienced drivers, to reverse around a corner. Vision is restricted, and the driving position adopted is anything but natural. It's an exercise calling for plenty of practice before the test to ensure that you can carry it out with the required degree of safety and accuracy.

Reversing into a restricted opening to the left is the usual form this manoeuvre takes, although drivers of van-type vehicles – which can include motor caravans or mini-buses – will probably be asked to reverse into a restricted opening on the right instead, in deference to the greater safety it gives in a vehicle already made difficult by the restricted rearward view from the driving seat.

In both cases this part of the test will be carried out at some chosen point in the 'natural drive' section of the test route.

## Reversing to the left

The examiner will tell you in advance that he wishes you to pull up just before you reach the road he has selected. This preliminary stop isn't intended to make things difficult for you by including extra pulling-up and moving away routines – it's a safety measure, allowing both you and the examiner himself to check the road into which you are to reverse. He will only ask you to proceed with the next part of the drill if he is satisfied that it is safe for you to do so.

You will have drawn up with your nearside wheels some 15 to 18 inches from the kerb, carrying out all the normal checks involved on your approach. When stopping, you may have to strike a balance between the requirement not to park within 15m of a

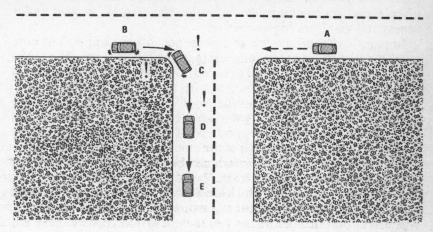

*Sequence for reversing to the left. A. On the approach, draw up 12in from the kerb, applying the normal routine; observe the road into which you are to reverse, noting any obstructions; then follow normal procedures for moving off to point beyond the junction. B. Draw up 18in from the kerb; check that indicators have cancelled; carry out visual check all round; if clear, engage reverse and move off; no signals. C. Turn into side road; remember that the front of the car will swing out, so check for traffic both ways and for pedestrians behind; continue if clear. D. Straighten up; drive parallel to the kerb, with clearance of 18in. E. Stop on examiner's instructions; engage handbrake and neutral. Watch the danger points = !*

junction and the need for both you and the examiner to be able to see clearly into the chosen road. Judge your pull-up so that you come to stop at the farthest point from the junction at which this is possible. Apply the handbrake, and select neutral.

Now assess the road into which you are to be asked to reverse. Your instructor will already have taught you to think of such corners in terms of angles – acute, moderately acute, and rounded are three typical descriptions, although some driving schools may use different appellations, such as sharp and semi-sharp. They all mean the same, though. An acute or sharp corner is one where the kerbstone is virtually a right-angle with the edge only a short radius. A moderately acute or semi-sharp corner has more of a sweep to it – the sort of entry that you often find at the approach end of a close of houses, for example. Rounded corners have a pronounced sweep not unlike that of a large roundabout. They're often found on the entrances of industrial estates, to give easier access and exit lines for lorries.

Implant a mental picture of the corner in your mind, and note anything that might entail some extra difficulty – a drain close to the corner, that you would need to avoid; signs of gravel accumulation in the gutters that could interfere with the accuracy of your steering; a pronounced camber in the road you are to enter, for which allowance must be made. Any such factors have to be taken into account, and you can make good use of the few seconds you have, providing your observation is acute.

And it will be only a few seconds before the examiner – now satisfied that the exercise can safely go ahead – will start explaining that *this* is the road into which he wishes you to reverse. He will then instruct you to drive past it, stop, and then reverse into it. He will also tell you that he wishes you then to drive in reverse gear 'for some distance, keeping reasonably close to the kerb.'

How far is 'some distance'? And how close to the kerb is 'reasonably close'? Unfortunately, he won't specify. However, you do know what the Highway Code says – 'You must not reverse your vehicle for longer than is necessary' so he is unlikely to expect you to cover more than a few car lengths – 30 or 40 feet (10/12m) – before asking you to pull up. Don't stop till then, if only because if you do he'll probably ask you to reverse further and you'll have an extra moving off and stopping exercise to do! Of course, if there's another vehicle parked in the road you have a built-in limit. He won't expect or want you to back right up to it!

As for a reasonable clearance between yourself and the kerb, try to end up with your nearside wheels exactly the same distance from the kerb as they were when you started. That way you can't really be faulted, providing you allowed the right distance in the beginning.

But at the moment you are still on the 'wrong' side of the junction. Do a normal pulling away exercise – not overlooking the 'mirrors-signal-manoeuvre' routine – and drive to a position between one and two car-lengths from the corner around which you have to reverse. That means more 'mirrors - signals - manoeuvre' work in a very short roadspace, but it still has to be done.

Judge your pull-up point accurately – you don't want to go further in reverse than is absolutely necessary, but you do need a clean lead-in to the corner. Ideally, you should pull up as soon as the whole of the corner is clearly visible in the rear-view mirror.

Timing the operation is up to you – the examiner will give no further instructions until he wants you to stop reversing – so your checks must be meticulous. But you have a decision to make. As this is an exercise involving reversing, you are entitled to remove your seat belt if you wish. With an inertia reel belt it's probably not necessary, but if you have a static harness your movements would almost certainly be too restricted were it left buckled up.

Check visually all round. Use your mirrors and a visual check over your right shoulder to make sure that there is no traffic approaching from the rear. If there is, let it pass. Check both in front and behind that there are no pedestrians near your car, and no children on the pavement likely to run behind it as you reverse.

Try to establish a reference point that will help you. In some cars, the rear screen and quarters will be low enough for you to see the kerb from the driving seat for quite a distance. Note where it appears to cross the bottom of the rear screen. If you can keep it in the same relative position as you reverse, you will maintain a constant distance from the kerb. Otherwise, see if there is some other marker, further down the road, that might help.

You can now move off. Engage reverse gear, release the hand-brake, and get the car moving. Keep the speed low – not above walking pace – and *don't* use your indicators: they will only confuse. Your reversing lights show plainly enough what you are doing. You, meantime, will be controlling the car while looking over your left shoulder, watching for the line of the kerb through the rear screen and the nearside rear window, and keeping your eyes skinned for other traffic – especially anything suddenly appearing in the road you are about to enter. If anything does, you will have to stop, and return to your starting point.

Up to the moment when you wish to turn into the side road you may, quite safely, have placed your left arm along the rear of the passenger seat to brace yourself. But, when you make the turn itself, though you remain twisted to the left and looking backwards, you *must* get your left hand back on the wheel and keep it there until you have rounded the corner. Remember, too, that during the turn the front of your car will swing to the offside, so look right and check that the road you are leaving is still clear and that your turn will not endanger other traffic.

If the camber is severe you may need to help the car round with a little more throttle – don't overdo it! – and as you come clear of the corner re-establish your reference point on the new kerb and continue to reverse until asked to stop. Then apply the handbrake, engage neutral, face forward, replace your seat belt if you took it off, and if all went well breathe a sigh of deep relief . . .

## Reversing to the right

It's swings and roundabouts here. To be asked to reverse to the right involves a more complicated pull-up – you have to stop on the left for observation, just as for a left-reverse; then move away, with all the appropriate signals, and position yourself as for a right turn; then cross over into the opposite lane and draw up facing oncoming traffic. You have massive blind spots in this situation, so visual checks for other vehicles and for pedestrians must be even more than usually thorough. Once you move off in reverse, however, you have one great advantage – instead of performing contortions to see where you are going, you can simply look at the kerb directly, through your open window, and follow it round. The only snag is that the all-round check for vehicles and pedestrians at the turning point is more difficult, since your view to the left is likely to be seriously restricted.

Once you have straightened up, remember that at the end of the exercise you will have to move away again and pull up in a safe position on the left-hand side of the road. Extra manoeuvring space will be essential. If you are eventually to come to rest no closer to the junction than 15m, you will need to reverse at least 40m down to give yourself room in which to carry out the cross-over. The 'mirrors - signal - manoeuvre' routine, plus thorough visual all-round observation, is essential during this part of the test involving, as it does, a potentially dangerous manoeuvre.

## Reversing on hills

You are unlikely to be asked to reverse on a gradient, but doing so might become necessary during the test if, for example, a narrow road unsuitable for turning was blocked by an accident and the only possible exit was fairly close behind you.

The techniques are a mixture of those for normal reversing and for moving off on a hill. However, when reversing uphill the car will be trying to run forwards, and when reversing downhill the car will

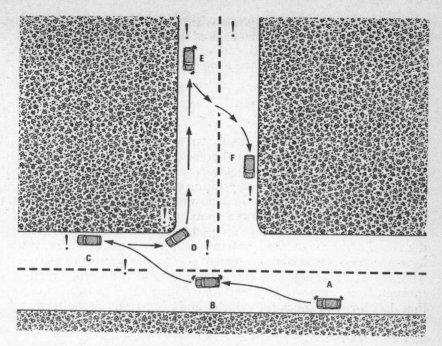

*Sequence for reversing to the right. A. Follow normal rountine, pull up 12in from the kerb on the approach; observe the road into which you are to reverse; check mirrors, signal right, move off. B. Check mirrors; align just to left of centre line; give way to approaching traffic; check right indicator on; move over to pull up alongside opposite kerb. C. Open driver's window as aid to reversing; check for approaching traffic; check for pedestrians in rear blind spots; check for traffic turning right; when clear, start to reverse. D. Turn parallel to the kerb; keep constant watch for pedestrians and other traffic; remember front of the car will swing out. E. Reverse well down road, keeping 12in from kerb. Check all round for traffic and pedestrians; signal left turn; move to opposite carriageway. F. Check mirrors; pull up 12in from kerb and at leat 15yd from junction; cancel indicators; engage handbrake and neutral. Pay particular attention to danger points = !*

be trying to run backwards. Apply the same rules as those for restarting forwards on gradients. If the car's tendency will be to move *opposite* the intended direction of travel, hold it on the handbrake as the clutch is released. If it wants to move *in* the direction of travel that is analogous to moving off on a down gradient, and the footbrake/clutch combination should be employed instead. Don't let the way the car is facing fool you! Just remember that in reversing the back of the car is now effectively the front and act accordingly.

# The Turn in the Road

Officially, it's a request to 'turn your car round in the road to face in the opposite direction, using forward and reverse gears.' In other words, an utterly precise way of saying 'Do a three-point turn.'

Of course, the popular name for this manoeuvre is a bit misleading. Under ideal circumstances, it is just what it implies – a turn involving just three moves. Starting from the nearside kerb, you turn across the road and stop at right-angles to the opposite kerbstone, your front bumber neatly in line with it, but not overhanging. Then, you reverse back to the opposite side, steering sharply left as you go, and stop again. This time, your car will be at an angle of 45 degrees to the line of the kerb, and the offside of your rear bumper will be exactly above the gutter but, again, not overhanging. You complete a textbook manoeuvre by once more driving across the road, turning right as you do so, to come straight ahead with the nearside of your car exactly 1m from the kerb enabling you to continue your journey without stopping.

And, indeed, it can be done like that – or could be, but for the 'ifs'. *If* the carriageway is wide enough. *If* your car's steering has sufficient lock. *If* the driver has first-rate judgement of distance. Unfortunately, these factors rarely coincide.

So, in practice, a three-point turn can involve more than three moves, and the possibility of that is recognised in the driving test requirement. Providing you do the turn safely and exhibit the required levels of control and judgement, you can make as many moves as you like – within reason.

Before looking at the techniques involved, let's consider some of the faults that would certainly count against you. The first is that familiar one – failure to pay sufficient attention to observation. This exercise involves a minimum of three manoeuvres across the carriageway, at least one of them in reverse. The potential dangers if you fail to observe other road users are obvious.

Next, on at least two of the moves your car will be moving towards the pavement. Misjudge your braking point, or lose control altogether, and the car might mount the pavement and hit a pedestrian. You will be specifically instructed *not* to touch the kerb, so it takes little imagination to guess what the examiner would be writing on his sheet were you actually to drive over it.

With some cars, you can infringe the footpath without the wheel actually touching the kerb at all. The overhang alone is enough to constitute a danger to pedestrians. This mainly applies to the reversing moves, and to saloon cars with large boots extending well beyond the rear wheels. There's little point in coming to a standstill with the offside rear wheel neatly positioned a foot from the kerb if a couple of feet of solid bodywork is then projecting over the pavement.

And, of course, the examiner will not have asked you to avoid touching the kerb *with your wheels*. He means 'with any part of your vehicle.' and that applies no matter in which direction you happen to be moving. So, just remember that many cars these days have deep air dams at the front, often a foot or more ahead of the wheels. Concentrating on placing the wheels in the right position, you may be startled to hear a loud scrunching noise from the front. That will be the air dam protesting as it is rammed into the kerb.

There's a potential kerb-snagger at the rear of your car too, ready to catch you out as you reverse. On some models – particularly the sportier cars in a range – the exhaust system is relatively low-mounted and the tail pipe projects almost to the line of the bumper. As you reverse towards the kerb, there's always a chance that the tailpipe and the kerbstone may be at exactly the same height (a risk all the greater if you are moving down a steep camber) and may meet noisily and, perhaps, expensively.

Control faults will almost certainly be penalised, and with so much manoeuvring involved there's plenty of scope for them. Smooth and proper use of the clutch is important. So, too, is the application of the handbrake at the end of each of the moves except the final one. Even there, if you have chosen to remove your seat belt you will be expected to stop and replace it before driving on – another need to apply the handbrake.

The examiner will also be watching your use of the steering, so be particularly careful not to go cross-armed in your efforts to change lock, and *never* try to turn the wheel while the car is stationary.

It is a peculiarity of this manoeuvre that you do *not* give signals when executing it, except as you are pulling up by the kerb and positioning yourself before beginning the exercise. Broadside across the carriageway at least twice, and not a single signal? Right. This is a clear-road manoeuvre, for a start – if the road isn't clear you don't begin – and if you attempted to signal during it the various light combinations would make your car a mobile rival to the Blackpool illuminations and twice as confusing. Right indicators on, then off. Left indicators and reversing lights on, then off. Right indicators on again. And perhaps one or two encores for luck. It's no wonder that the test specifically omits signalling here: so don't do it!

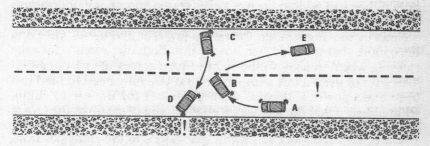

*Sequence for "three point turn" in road. A. Check mirrors, signal, pull up no more than 12in from kerb; check indicators cancelled; check for traffic and pedestrians in mirrors and by visual observation in blind spots; when safe, move forward, and then turn sharply right across road. B. Approaching centre line check right left right; stop if traffic approaches until sure of its intentions, then resume; if possible, tighten turn to right. C. After crossing centre line prepare to straighten up, applying left lock for last 4ft to the kerb; close towards kerb without touching and with no overhang; stop, engage handbrake and neutral; visual checks all round; if clear, move off in reverse, left lock applied; check for traffic before recrossing centre line. D. Continue to reverse, preparing to straighten up; when 4ft from kerb start applying right lock; stop near to kerb, but without touching or overhang; engage handbrake and neutral; visual observation all round. When safe to do so, engage first gear, release handbrake, and drive forward on right lock. E. Straighten up and continue to drive 1m from kerb; if seat belt was removed, check mirrors, signal left, pull in, stop, and replace it. All points marked "!" are potential dangers.*

Start by selecting your pulling-up point. If possible, after being asked by the examiner to pull up at a convenient point, choose a spot with as little camber as possible, clear of any obstructions.

Follow the normal routine for pulling up at the kerb ('mirrors - signal - manoeuvre') and make sure that you stop as near to the kerb as you reasonably can to give the maximum road space for the turn. Don't cut it too fine though: there's no point in gaining an extra few inches of road width if you risk hitting the kerb on the easiest part of the exercise. Follow the usual sequence after stopping – handbrake on, select neutral.

Now wind your window down. There are two reasons for this. One is that you can look behind into your blind spot by putting your head out. Do that after you have prepared to move off with the usual 'mirror-signal-manoeuvre' routine and a visual check to front and rear and both sides. Then check your blind spot, and move off only if the road is clear both of other traffic and of any pedestrians who may wish to cross nearby.

Start by moving straight forward a few feet and then – checking once more that the road remains clear in both directions – turn the steering wheel quickly to the right to turn across the carriageway. This isn't in itself a fast manoeuvre, but you may need to feed in a little extra power if there is a steep camber for the car to climb. Remember, if you do, to ease off again as you come up to the crown of the road.

Let the car continue to turn to the right as you cross the centre line, and keep the speed low, and slowing, as you approach the kerb. When it is about 5ft ahead of you, quickly start turning the wheel to the left. You want, at least, to have the front wheels pointing straight ahead as you brake to a standstill. If you have enough road space to win a little left lock in the final foot or so, all well and good. In some instances, where the car is relatively short and the road wider than usual you may even be able to wind on full left lock. Concentrate, however, on coming to rest with no part of the nose of the car overhanging the kerb, but as close as you can get otherwise. Apply the handbrake and select neutral.

That's the first part out of the way, but don't rest on your laurels. Look right, then left, then right again – and behind too. Then, if all is still clear, engage reverse, bring the clutch to biting point, and hold the car on the handbrake as you give a little power, and gradually let the clutch take up. Release the brake as you do so. Quickly apply left lock as the car gathers way.

This time, you're reversing in a way that enables you really to see where you're going (at least part of the time) by putting your head through the window and looking back along the side of the car. But remember, you can't do it this way if you car is still angled to your right when you start. Then, you'll need to look behind your left shoulder until the angle changes. As the car reaches the point at which it is straight across the carriageway, you can stop looking over the left shoulder and begin looking over the right.

Looking out through the window gives a better view for judging distance, and absolutely clear vision of any traffic or pedestrians approaching from your right. But, it also means that the whole bulk of the car is between you and anything that is happening behind and to your left. So, don't become over-entranced by the view through that open window. Check to the left of the car and in the mirrors behind as well – popping your head out again as you come closer to the kerb.

By now, the car should have crossed the centre line, so be ready to prevent it from accelerating down the camber. Keep it on left lock until you can see that the offside corner of the car – the nearest part to the kerb – is about six feet (2m) away from the edge of the road, quickly turn the wheel to the right and continue easing backwards. Judge it correctly and you should be able to brake to a standstill with no part of your car overhanging the kerb, but with plenty of road in front of you into which to make your final turn.

Remember the drill, though. On coming to a stop, apply the handbrake, engage neutral, and put your left hand back on the wheel while you again check for safety – right, left, right; mirrors and glances over your shoulders for the blind spots behind.

Move off again as before, continuing to turn the wheel to the right. If you can turn the car smoothly on to the correct line for driving away in the opposite direction by all means do so, but don't try to force it to happen. There's nothing to be gained by running smartly into the opposite kerb with full right lock still applied.

If there simply isn't room, just follow the same sequence as before – cross the centre-line, turning right. Slow. Approach the kerb, turning the wheel left from six feet out. Stop. Handbrake on and engage neutral. Safety checks right, left, right, behind. Engage reverse and do another leg across the carriageway. Another stop. More checks – and a final leg out.

On this last turn, your aim should be to end up facing in the opposite direction, with your nearside wheels a good metre from the kerb. If you do that, and you hadn't removed your seat belt, then you can simply continue to drive ahead until the examiner (or road signs, or markings) give you another direction to follow. But if you did decide to take your belt off then as soon as your car is again straight you must pull up (adhering to the routine) and replace it.

Some examiners may expect you to stop the engine after pulling up, then fit your belt, then do a full 'restart and move off' sequence.

Hopefully, on a quiet road you will have time to complete your 'three-point turn' without interruption. If, however, another vehicle approaches while you are carrying it out the golden rule is to stop, wait, and let the other driver make his intentions clear before you proceed. If in doubt, give way – and then don't move until it is safe to do so.

# Turning the Corner

Defining the requirements for negotiating turns and corners is simple enough. You need to approach at the right speed, in the right gear, on the right part of the road; take a line through the corner that will result in the car emerging still at the right speed, in the right gear, and on the right part of the road. And you need to know, having got all *that* right, that where you have been unsighted you are still able to stop within the distance you can see to be clear.

As a learner, you have one other problem: you have to satisfy the examiner sitting tight-lipped beside you that you did in fact get it all right. So don't try to corner like Nigel Mansell mounting a charge – *he* doesn't have to worry about traffic coming the other way, nor is he likely to encounter a tractor drawing some farm implement bedecked with spikes like a medieval instrument of torture just round the next blind bend. You do, and may.

Of course, it's equally unlikely that you will be travelling at 140mph . . .

## Turn left

The first turn you will probably be asked to make is one to the left. It may be a side turning, or it may be a road junction, but the procedure is much the same.

We can take it for granted that you will be driving steadily along a more or less straight stretch of road, the car neatly positioned no more than 1m from the kerb, the speed held – according to conditions – at between 20 and 30mph. That presupposes that you will be using either third or fourth gear.

On being instructed to turn left, obviously, your first action must be to identify the road into which you are to turn. If there are several side turnings, the examiner will be explicit – 'the second road on the left', for example – so you need have no fears that you will blot your copybook by haring off down the wrong turning.

Take a good, hard look ahead. Are there any road signs or road markings that must be obeyed? Is your approach made more difficult by parked vehicles that demand the appropriate clearance? Are there pedestrians walking up the pavement towards the road into which you have to turn? If so, will they be likely to cross it? If so, you will have to be prepared to give way.

With the approach duly weighed up, you are clear to start your normal routine of 'mirrors - signal - manoeuvre'. Be particularly careful to check what is happening on your nearside, because it's here that a cyclist or motorcyclist may be partially hidden from view. Your nearside door mirror should tell you, but it could be worth a glance over your left shoulder just to make sure. And though your interior mirror and offside door mirror will pick up traffic behind you or holding back to the right, they won't show up the car that is already up to your rear quarter and overtaking. Check over your right shoulder.

All clear? Then it's eyes front and operate the nearside indicator to show that you intend to turn left. Hold a steady course, still with your 1m clearance, and start to brake gently to reduce speed to what you judge to be appropriate for turning the corner. A right-angle turn can be done quite happily at about 20mph, but the examiner might think that a bit fast for a learner. So reduce speed to 15mph – lower if you're not too happy about it – and engage second gear to give yourself adequate throttle control and a modicum of engine braking.

As you come to the point at which you can see into the road that you are joining, look ahead for possible hazards, and decide how you propose to deal with them. If there are vehicles parked near the junction, for instance, you know that you will have to allow adequate clearance for passing them, and there's no point in swinging round on a line that will put you a metre from the kerb if you then have to pull out again to miss them. You'll need to straighten up at a distance of 'one average car's width plus one metre' from the kerb instead. Allow that an average car is two metres wide, add your safe metre clearance, and aim to turn on a radius that will bring you into the new road three metres from the kerb, with no need to dog-leg round the obstruction.

So, you've got it all planned – all you need to do now is turn the steering wheel. Well, almost all. There's no need to slam on full left lock – you'll only find yourself climbing the pavement if you do! – but the movement of the wheel must be sufficient to ensure that the car doesn't wander off to the right over the centre line. Either of those would be marked as a dangerous fault, and quite right too. Instead, follow the line of the kerb and keep it cutting your bonnet at the point that you already know indicates a one-metre kerb clearance. As a guide, most cars will require between one turn and one and three-quarters turns of the wheel, depending on the gearing of the steering mechanism and the required radius to turn. Full lock usually involves three to three and a half turns of the wheel from lock to lock.

If there's nothing to avoid, progressively wind off the lock as the car rounds the corner, and as it straightens out centralise the wheel and apply pressure as necessary against the camber. Accelerate gently back to your normal cruising speed, and select the appropriate gear. Check that your indicator has cancelled.

If you are coming further out into the road to avoid obstructions, initiate your turn at the same point, but with a little less lock applied so that the car continues to move out towards the centre line. Don't let it cross: your aim is to make a smooth, constant-radius sweep into the clear part of the road, ending up with just the right clearance to your left to allow you to go straight ahead until you have passed the obstruction. Then apply 'the routine' and regain your correct position a metre out from the kerb.

## Left at a junction

Same thing, only different – because this time you will either have to stop or, at the least, be prepared to give way. Road signs and road markings will give you the necessary instructions.

Although the actual mechanics of a left turn from a junction are not over-complicated, the quality of observation is all-important.

On the approach, follow your well-established 'mirrors-signal-manoeuvre' routine, slowing under gentle braking to come to a halt in the left-hand lane, one metre from the kerb. Apply the handbrake, engage neutral, and double-check that you are still indicating a turn to the left.

Now comes the point at which so many learners fail the test – observation, and drawing the correct conclusion from what is seen has to be balanced against the need to avoid 'undue hesitancy'. You may think that this is a classic case of 'heads I lose, tails I lose.'

Look to your right, to check on approaching traffic. Look to your left, to weigh up the road into which you are turning, and assess the likely actions of traffic from the other direction. Then look right again. If you are not satisfied that it is safe to move out you must stay where you are, and continue visual checks. Right-left-right. You must be sure that when you move off you will not endanger or inconvenience other road users.

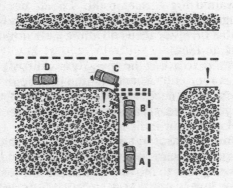

*Sequence for a left turn on to a major road. A. Position the car 1m from the kerb; check mirrors, signal, brake. B. Observe traffic and pedestrians; give way to traffic on the major road. Keep signalling left. C. If clear, proceed. Follow the line of the kerb at 1m distance, indicators still on. D. Straighten up, still 1m from the kerb, and drive on. Check indicators have cancelled. ! = danger point.*

So what are you looking for? To your right, approaching vehicles. You have to assess their course and their speed. To your left, pedestrians crossing or obviously about to cross the road into which you are to turn – plus any obvious hazards such as parked cars, especially any that may be on the point of pulling out from the kerb. Regard with grave suspicion any parked vehicle whose driving seat is occupied. If you can see smoke from its exhaust pipe, then the engine is running and it could pull out unexpectedly just as you've committed yourself. Don't take the absence of a signal as an indication that it won't do so – some drivers operate their indicators only at the last moment; sometimes not at all.

The main dangers, though, lie to the right. How far down the road can you see? If this is a built-up area, lamp-posts will be 200 yards apart at the most – but usually only 40 or 50 yards. Traffic will certainly be moving at 30mph, at least. That's 44 feet per second, so if there's a lamp-post near you and if an approaching car is just passing the second lamp-post within your range of vision you have at best 15 seconds before it reaches the junction. Well, you could just make it – allow 3 seconds for moving off, and another 6 seconds in which to accelerate to 30mph, but the examiner might be underwhelmed if you drove out in front of a moving vehicle when you could have waited for a clear road. The choice is yours – is 15 seconds enough to justify a verdict of 'undue hesitancy'? Possibly, but that's probably better than collecting a moving car through your door, so wait and simply murmur (rather loudly) to yourself 'I believe that car's exceeding the speed limit. I'll play safe and let him pass.' Then, as soon as it clears the junction, look right, left, right again. If the road is now clear for a good 300 yards engage first gear, lift off the handbrake, check in your mirrors and over your shoulder, and go.

Of course, the vehicle that's approaching may be indicating a left turn itself. Don't be misled by that – drivers have been known not to cancel their indicators, so treat it with grave suspicion. Wait until it has actually turned into 'your' road before you move. Don't under any circumstances start off while it is still turning, because it will be completely blocking your view of the approach of other traffic. You could find yourself half-way through your turn with a motorcycle, which squeezed past the tail of the turning vehicle, moving fast towards you on a collision course.

Always remember that anything nearby on the road to your right will reduce your range of vision. Even a couple of people chatting on the pavement can form a remarkably effective screen. Don't be tempted to pull forward to look round them if there is a solid white 'Stop' line on the road. In the absence of a 'Stop' line, it is normally in order, though, to creep slowly forward to obtain a better view.

Once you've decided that it's 'all systems go', the rest of the operation is simple enough – a combination of moving away from a standstill and a left-hand turn.

## Turn right

Here the manoeuvre is not as simple as a turn to the left. Firstly, you must position the car accurately, with its wheels just to the left of the centre-line, on the final approach to the junction. All the precautions involved in an approach for a left turn apply, but in addition you have to time your move to just left of the centre of the road accurately, and carry out the full 'mirrors-signal-manoeuvre' routine far enough away from the turning point not to inconvenience following traffic. It is particularly important that you should check over your shoulder into your blind spot on the right before moving off your original driving line closer to the kerb.

Be particularly careful to check that, once you have straightened up on the new line, your right indicator has not cancelled itself. If it has, you'll need to initiate the 'turn right' signal once again – but, if you do, don't forget your mirror check first.

On the approach, you will need to observe approaching vehicles. If a car from the other direction is indicating a left turn into the road you are planning to enter, don't try to race it. Give way, slowing to a stop if necessary.

There may be a vehicle standing in the left-hand carriageway of the same road, signalling an intention to turn right. Is it going to drive out in front of you? Be prepared to slow or stop, just in case. Check on the road markings. Is the onus on the other driver to give way to you? If there is a 'stop' line across his carriageway at that point, or the broken 'give way' road marking, then he should allow priority while you, on the major road, should not inconvenience following traffic by stopping. But be suspicious, nonetheless.

As soon as you can see clearly into the road to your right, look – as in a left turn – for any hazards or obstructions. Remember, in particular, that it is up to you to give way to any pedestrian who is actually crossing the road at the junction.

Approaching traffic displaying no signals has to be taken into account. Slow down, and stop if necessary to allow it to pass. Driving in front of a moving vehicle is a gamble not worth the taking.

The turn itself, once you have ample time and road space, is simplicity itself, for you have a commanding view of the road you are leaving and of the road you are entering. But don't think that mistakes aren't possible. They are – and the worst one you can make is to 'cut the corner' by putting your offside wheels over the centre-line and into the opposite carriageway as you enter the new road.

Your aim must be to enter cleanly, keeping your car just to the left of the centre line, subsequently moving on to your normal cruise position a metre from the kerb. If you can see that the road is clear of obstructions, you can start your right turn a little later and swing round straight on to a course that will bring you out on that line without the need for subsequent alteration. If you do so, though, you must be very careful indeed not to misjudge your turn-off point. Leave the turn too late, and you won't have space in which to complete it without, at best, having to 'dog-leg' the car hard right and then left to enter the road at all. In the very worst case, you will simply end up across the carriageway with nothing in front of you but pavement and nothing beside you but a furiously scribbling examiner . . .

## Turn right at a junction

Again, the same in theory as turning left at a junction, but with the added complication that you have to cross one carriageway and enter another – which gives you *two* lines of moving traffic to contend with.

Concentrate, first, on positioning your car properly. Move to a position just left of the centre line (remember 'the routine', and the

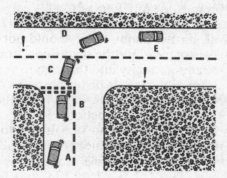

*Sequence for a right turn on to a major road. A. Position the car 1m from the kerb. Check mirrors, signal right, move just to left of centre line. Brake. B. Observe traffic and pedestrians; give way to traffic on major road in both directions. Right indicators still on. C. When safe, drive straight ahead towards centre line of major road. Check again for traffic. Right indicators still on. D. Turn right when safe; accelerate; right indicators still on. E. Resume normal cruise 1m from kerb; check indicators off. != danger point.*

subsequent check on your indicators to ensure they're still signal-ling a right turn. Brake gently to a standstill, engage the handbrake; engage neutral.

Now, just as for a left turn, concentrate on what's happening in the road to your right, and what obstructions or hazards there are in the road into which you are to turn. Plan your driving to take account of them.

Wait until you can see that there is a safe gap in the traffic pattern on your right. Then weigh up the situation on the left. You are waiting not just for one safe gap, but for two – and until you get them you must be prepared to wait. You will undoubtedly have seen experienced drivers nose out and then wait, halfway across the carriageway, to tuck into the opposing traffic stream. Don't try to emulate them: you need to make this turn in one move. And blocking half a road isn't really consistent with 'not inconveniencing other road users' anyway.

As soon as your two safe gaps coincide, quickly check right-left-right. Check your mirrors, your indicators – and then manoeuvre! Accelerate towards the crown of the road. Slow down as you approach it, apply the requisite amount of right lock on the steering – again, one to one and threequarter turns should suffice – and turn on a constant radius either just to the left of the centre-line or into the cruise position a metre from the kerb, as circumstances demand.

Straighten up, check your indicators have cancelled, and resume natural driving.

## Controlled crossings

How easy life becomes when you have traffic lights or an understanding police officer to help you, you may think. And certainly a controlled left turn *is* easy. Just make your signals, give way to pedestrians crossing the road you wish to enter, make sure your positioning is accurate, and you should have no problems.

But turning right can be a different matter. The green light that permits you to proceed providing it is safe to do so gives exactly the same permission to traffic in the opposing carriageway. From your position in the right-hand lane, therefore, you have to assess their intentions and make the appropriate allowances.

Obviously, you cannot turn right while traffic from the opposite direction is proceeding straight ahead. If you are the lead car in the right-hand lane, though, it is usually deemed permissible for you to move forward, line up between the traffic islands, and to wait there for a safe gap to materialise, or for the lights to change so that you can complete your turn to the right. On the other hand, the

Highway Code *does* say that you should not move on to the junction unless your exit is clear. With traffic pouring past from the opposite direction, demonstrably it is *not* clear. Therefore, strictly speaking, you should remain stationary until it is.

It's a point on which different instructors appear to have different ideas – perhaps based on knowledge of what their local examiners expect – so the best advice in this case is to follow whatever procedure you have learned. If it is to move forward, however, do try to keep your car as far to the right as you can, and as nearly parallel to the centre-line as possible, so that traffic behind that wishes to drive straight ahead can do so.

A second complication is what to do if a car in the opposing traffic stream wishes to turn right and has decided to 'hook' – that is, turns sharply right and stops, so that if you wish to join him in the middle of the junction you will have to do so nearside to nearside. 'Hooking', frankly, is plain bad driving: unfortunately, bad driving that is given an official seal of approval by some road authorities who paint arrows on the road to encourage it. One suspects that the county surveyors responsible are unfit to drive even a horse and cart. Or have never driven anything else!

However, if you wish to turn right at all without sitting out another sequence of traffic lights, and then perhaps with just the same result, you may have little choice but to join the idiot there. Your examiner, after all, may be hooked on 'hooking' and not on 'undue hesitancy', and *he* doesn't have to give reasons for any of his whims. So – unless your instructor has specifically taught you otherwise – move off and turn to your right to come to rest beside the other car, allowing reasonable clearance. You now have no option but to wait for the lights to change, because the car to your left will completely block your view of approaching traffic, and until it is stopped you *must not* move.

Once it is safe to do so, check your mirrors, look right, left, right, and carry out a normal right-turn routine. If you've been forced to hook, remember that you will not be in the ideal position to make a cleanly radiused turn. Depending on circumstances, it may be advisable to run straight for a yard or two, and then apply lock that will take you on to the correct position on the road you are entering.

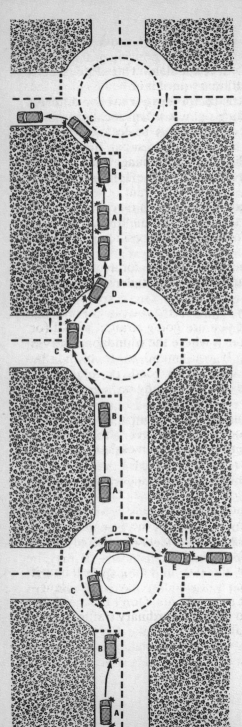

*Sequence for turning left at roundabout. A. Position the car 1m from the kerb; check mirrors; brake. B. Check mirrors again; stop at "Give way" markings if traffic is on the roundabout to your right; indicate left turn; proceed when safe. C. Check road into which you intend to turn; check mirrors; check left indicator on; follow road round to left. D. Resume straight drive 1m from kerb; check indicators cancelled. At "!", watch for vehicles not signalling – they may intend to cross to the same exit as yourself.*

*Sequence for going straight ahead at roundabout. A. Position the car 1m from the kerb; check mirrors; slow; no signals. B. Observe across the roundabout for obstructions; give way to traffic from the right; when clear, proceed; still no signals. C. Begin signalling a left turn as you pass this exit, first checking your mirrors. D. Turn into the exit road; left indicator still on. E. Drive on 1m from kerb; check indicators off. Danger pionts = !*

*Sequence for turning right at roundabout. A. Position the car 1m from the kerb; check mirrors; signal right turn; move to just left of centre line; brake. B. Observation; give way to traffic from right; proceed when clear; right indicator still on. C. Follow right hand lane; check right indicator still on; check mirrors and watch for traffic overtaking on your left. D. When passing exit before the one you wish to take check mirrors; signal a left turn. E. Turn left, selecting the appropriate lane. F. Drive on 1m from the kerb; check indicators off. "!" = danger point.*

# Turns at roundabouts

Although described as 'turns', on a roundabout of any size the actions are more appropriate to those required for bends. Only the left turn is a true turn. Going straight on means that you actually negotiate a shallow S-bend; turning right, a sharp one.

When positioning for a turn at a roundabout, select the appropriate lane, apply 'the routine' – and then remember that drivers behind you may not be so punctilious and may change lanes without warning. So make frequent mirror checks on the approach. Don't let them distract you, however, from the constant observation of the roundabout itself, and the exit you intend to take.

On a two-lane approach, use the left-hand lane if you intend to turn left or go straight ahead. For a right turn position yourself in the right-hand lane.

If there are three lanes, use the left-hand lane for a left turn; the centre lane for straight ahead; and, again, the right-hand lane for turning right.

Signals are important. Initially, signal left if you plan to take the first exit; give no initial signal if you are going straight ahead (or taking a turning beyond the first exit where the roundabout serves more than three other roads). If you intend to go round the roundabout, either to turn off on another road, or to join the opposite carriageway of the road you are already on, signal a right turn.

Give way to traffic on the roundabout to your right, and then perform the appropriate manoeuvre. The left turn is simple enough. When going straight ahead (or taking an earlier turning to the left) don't forget to indicate a left turn just as you pass the turning immediately *before* the one you intend to take. Remember that you are effectively turning left in either case. Therefore, you should keep to the left-hand lane throughout and not attempt to 'straight-line' the roundabout by starting in the left-hand lane, cutting across the right-hand lane of the roundabout, and then across to the left-hand lane on the exit.

You may, however, go straight ahead from the right-hand lane if the left-hand lane on the approach is blocked by, say, an accident – a lot of 'shunts' tend to happen at roundabouts. Don't use the right-hand lane simply in an attempt to 'jump' an ordinary traffic queue.

When going *round* the roundabout (i.e. to take any exit to the right of the road straight ahead of you) keep signalling a right turn, changing to a left turn signal just as you pass the exit immediately before the one you intend to take. Try to make your turn so that you can immediately adopt your normal cruise position. If your exit has one lane obstructed, however, make your turn gentler and allow the car to enter the new road just to the left of the centre-line, then carry out 'the routine' when you are clear to take up a position a metre from the kerb.

While you are on the roundabout, keep checking your mirrors. This is one of the few places where traffic is permitted to overtake on the left, and you may find somebody trying to pass you just at the point where you yourself wish to turn left. If so, slow and give way, then continue your turn when there is no longer any danger of a collision. Be particularly careful to check for motorcycles on your left – they are small enough to be missed in your mirrors, so a glance over your left shoulder is absolutely essential before you turn.

Just the same rules apply at mini-roundabouts. Don't bump the car over the central hump – you're supposed to go round the thing, not over it! – and watch out for the odd impatient driver who wants to go straight on and simply straightlines on the wrong side. They do exist . . .

# Overtaking, Speed and Pace

By virtue both of its likely location and its relatively short allotted time, the driving test should involve little, if any, overtaking. A typical example – passing a slow-moving milk float – was cited and you are unlikely to have to pass anything but slow-moving or stationary vehicles in a normal urban test run.

But you never can tell – you *may* have to do it, so you also have to know how to do it safely.

Let's consider the worst possible case. In an area with a 40mph limit you are travelling close to the legal maximum and closing on a vehicle ahead whose speed you estimate to be no more than 25mph. You are on a straight stretch of road, but you can see that about a quarter of a mile ahead it bends to the left. Should you overtake or not? Come to that, *could* you overtake safely or not?

You are faced with a problem of relative speeds. The car you are overhauling is a driving school hatchback, 15 feet long. Your speed relative to it is your 40mph, less its 25mph, so if you overtake it will be at a relative speed of only 15mph.

But that car is longer than you think, assuming that you are going to leave adequate safety clearances. You should not come closer to it on your present course than the two-second rule allows – one yard clearance per mile per hour. At your 15mph relative speed, that means allowing a clearance of 45 feet, and when you overtake you must leave that same clearance in front. You have to allow for your own car's 15-foot length too – clearance is measured from the *back* of your vehicle, not the front, after overtaking.

So the *effective* length of the car you may wish to overtake is not just 15 feet, but 45 feet rear clearance, 15 feet for the car itself, 45 feet for front separation, and the 15 feet of your own car. That makes a total of 120 feet (36m). At that relative speed of 15mph you are travelling at 22 feet per second, so it will take you a minimum of 5½ seconds to overtake and regain your position on the road from the time that you have pulled out.

However, your car's true speed is *not* 15mph: it is 40 mph – 58.7 feet per second. So, in 5 ½ seconds you will use up 323 feet (98m) of road space. On a clear road, you should be able to overtake safely, with plenty of road still in hand before you reach the bend.

But what if there happens to be a car coming the other way, hidden from you by the bend? If it, too, is travelling at 40mph, it will cover the same distance as you in your overtaking time. And you must allow it the same safety clearance – a two-second separation at least – to be sure that you won't have a head-on collision on your hands. How far would it travel in 7½ seconds? Multiply 58.7 feet per second by 7 ½, and you get 440 feet (134m). Add your own overtaking distance of 323 feet (98m) and you find that you need 763 feet (232m) of clear road to be safe.

So, assuming that you have estimated the distance to the bend accurately, and that whoever comes round it is not exceeding the 40mph limit, you can be home and dry with a comfortable 559 ft (170m) in hand. That shouldn't turn the examiner's hair grey prematurely, so you decide to pass.

You are already closing to the proper separation distance, and maintaining your speed in the appropriate gear (probably third), so you carry out 'the routine' and place your car just to the left of the centre line. Then you check behind you again – including a glance over your shoulder into the blind spot – and look well ahead, past the other car. All is still clear, and both vehicles are holding their constant speed, so you signal that you are pulling out to the right, and commence overtaking. Allow a good metre of clearance between the nearest point of your nearside and the other car's offside – don't forget those protruding door mirrors on both vehicles. You have to allow, also, for the possibility that the other car (it's driven by a fellow-learner, remember) might swerve.

As the rear of your car comes level with the front of the overtaken vehicle, start counting. The best way is to say to yourself silently 'Only a fool breaks the two-second rule' – which, spoken normally, takes two seconds to complete. Then check in your mirrors, change your signal from right turn to left turn, and move back into your normal position a metre from the kerb. Don't cut in – as we advised (in chapter eight) aim to regain position by slanting in at about 30 degrees and then straightening up.

If your judgement was correct you should now be about 170m

from the bend which, you estimate, can be taken safely at 30mph. So you check once again in your mirrors to ensure that the car you have just overtaken is still dropping back, and about 100m from the bend you brake gently to the appropriate speed, change gear if you think it necessary to do so – most cars would still be happy in third – and take the corner in a clean sweep, maintaining your position of the road and looking through the bend to ensure that there are no obstructions.

By any normal standards it would be a harsh examiner indeed who would fail you for an overtaking manoeuvre such as the one just described – the alternative course of reducing speed to 25mph and following the other car for perhaps half a mile could equally well have you black-marked for 'undue hesitancy' – providing you took action in good time, followed 'the routine' to the letter, didn't cut in, didn't exceed the speed limit, and inconvenienced or endangered nobody.

However, given the same scenario with a subtle difference, you *could* have failed.

Suppose that you hadn't noticed a car parked on the nearside – perhaps hidden from your immediate line of vision by the car you wished to overtake. Obviously, the car in front would have to pull out to avoid it – either that or slow down, perhaps stop, as you carried out your manoeuvre. That driver *would* have been inconvenienced and, as a learner, perhaps even endangered. Did you take the precaution of looking *through* the vehicle ahead (or even along its nearside, when you were far enough behind it to do so) to ensure that *both* sides of the road were clear?

Or what if there had been a car parked on the opposite side of the road with the driver already in his seat? Might that have pulled out unexpectedly before you had finished overtaking, so creating a dangerous situation? What if there had been side turnings, from which a vehicle might suddenly have swung in front of you? Did you check that they were clear? Were you sure that you could complete your manoeuvre before you reached them? All these things are matters of supposition and individual assessment – facts of life that make it impossible for any instructor (or any book!) to guarantee you a first-time pass.

The best advice on overtaking during the test is to ask, first, 'Is it necessary?' Then ask 'Is it safe?'. If the answer to both cases is 'Yes' then you have *got* to do it; but if you can honestly say 'No' to either question, be content to stay behind.

# Once you've passed

No, not passed a car but passed the test! Suddenly, you will be in the real world. You will be no more experienced than you were hardly an hour ago, but you will not now have the limited protection from other drivers that your L-plates afforded, and there may be occasions when you will heartily wish you still had them – at least they made other drivers steer clear of you.

Now you will find that the generality of drivers who wish to overtake you won't observe all the niceties of clearances and positioning to which you have accustomed yourself. You will have to get used to faster cars – much faster cars – closing to with a few feet of your rear bumper and then, with perhaps a cautionary flash of headlamps, pulling out sharply to overtake, only to cut in equally sharply into your carefully-preserved braking distance gap.

Don't be tempted to copy them, because the mathematics of overtaking remain constant. The safest way to overtake is also the quickest way to overtake *within the limits allowed by law*. So always try to pass from a constant speed, as near to that limit as the law allows.

You'll find that, most of the time, you will not be able to establish a great speed differential between yourself and the vehicle you are overtaking. It'll be a relative speed of 20mph, at best.

Let's take a look at an open-road situation similar to that postulated earlier in this chapter. But we'll make the road subject to a 60mph limit; we'll make the overtaken vehicle a 40ft juggernaut travelling at 40mph; and we'll see just how it all works out in practice.

Visualise that juggernaut as towing behind it a box junction into which you cannot enter, and pushing another one ahead of it. You are approaching from the rear at 60mph, and you therefore have to allow a separation equivalent to twice the distance you would cover in two seconds at your relative speed of 20mph. In round figures, that's 60 feet (18m). To that, add the length of the juggernaut (40ft) and the same two-second separation at a relative 20mph ahead of it – another 60 feet. Lastly, add the length of your car – 15ft – and the effective length of the moving obstruction is 175 ft (53m). At a relative speed of 20mph (60mph – 40mph) the complete overtaking manoeuvre will take you six seconds to complete. In that time, at 60mph, your car will travel 528 ft (161m).

Just as with the other road in our example, there is a left-hand bend some 400m down the road, round which approaching traffic

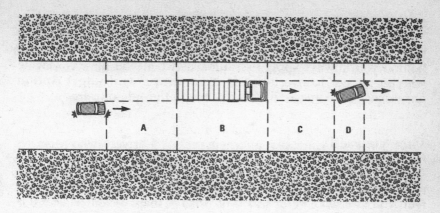

*Overtaking a moving vehicle. A. Do not encroach on this safety distance.*
*B. Assess the length of the overtaken vehicle; a car will be about 15ft long,*
*a heavy goods vehicle 40ft or more. C. Do not enter this safety distance.*
*D. Return to the nearside without cutting in.*

might come. If a car from the opposite direction rounds that corner just as you are committed, do you still have time to complete overtaking safely?

Add on the necessary two-second separation, and you have a time of eight seconds, during which it will travel 704 feet (214m). You need 161m yourself, making a total distance of 376m.

That's cutting it pretty fine, though – because on the open road you cannot assume that traffic will be obeying speed limits. On a road with 60mph limit, it's safer to assume that the traffic coming towards you will be moving at 70mph, not 60mph. If so, it will cover not 214m, but 250m. Add your necessary 161m, and you could find yourself in an uncomfortable head-to-head situation, with 411m needed and only 400m in hand . . .

Theoretical situations, not typical of day-to-day motoring? Perhaps. In the real world, away from the artificial constraints of the driving test, there is far more cut and thrust – and we have the accident statistics to prove it! Separation distances are *not* regarded as sacrosanct. Drivers *do* cut in shortly after overtaking. Approaching drivers – unless possessed by a death wish – *do* brake and give way, or pull over to allow room. True, it's not often done with very good grace, and they have ways of displaying their displeasure. But, again, too often for comfort, somebody makes a bad error of judgement. One or two more casualties are added to the statistics, and the lives of one or two more families suddenly collapse in ruins.

Overtaking is one of the most dangerous of all manoeuvres and it must be approached with caution. Even when the test may be long behind you, always apply its standards when you have to decide whether or not to overtake. 'Is it necessary? Is it safe?' And in answering those questions, always err on the side of caution.

## Pace yourself

The main lesson that can be learned from the driving test is the exercise of caution. If everybody were to drive as if that silent, watchful examiner were still occupying the front passenger seat it is doubtful if traffic would move much more slowly than it does now, but it would certainly move more safely.

Freed from your L-plates you may be tempted to let your natural exuberance take over, and develop a leaden throttle foot.

Don't. It isn't speed that gets you from point to point quickly: it's smooth, safe driving that does the trick by enabling you to maintain a brisk, even pace.

Mere speed offers diminishing returns. Take, as an example, a 50-mile trip – about the average for most people. At a modest average speed of 45mph, it takes 67 minutes to complete. Put the average up to 50mph – still within the compass of the average driver in an average car, and it can be done in one hour flat. That's a saving of seven minutes.

Now raise the average to 55mph. Here, you'll find yourself working rather harder, making full use of your opportunities but still not taking chances. But your return is already diminishing: a journey time of 54 minutes offers only a six-minute saving.

An average of 60mph is far, far harder to maintain. Now, you would almost certainly be striving right to the limit (in more ways than one) and your passengers would not be enjoying the trip. Your reward? Fifty minutes from start to finish, and only a niggardly four further minutes saved.

There's no need to go higher up the scale – except on motorways, it simply isn't possible to average 65mph for 50 miles and still stay within the law. Even if it could be done, the extra time saving is by now down to less than four minutes.

Oddly enough, the lower speeds usually prove to be just as quick in the long run. Faster cars tend to lose more time when baulked by traffic, and experience shows that the best way to make progress is to go up to the legal limit for the particular road you are on, and hold it as long as it is safe to do so. More ground can be gained by applying anticipation of road conditions ahead, and positioning the car accordingly, rather than by driving faster only to be forced to constantly decelerate and then accelerate again.

On a really long run of, say, 300 miles, holding a steady cruising speed can actually be a time-saver, since all cars return a far better fuel consumption under such conditions. True, your mate with the leaden foot may disappear over the horizon for a while, but you'll usually spot him stationary at the pumps before the trip's over. Since even a quick refill can take five minutes or more – remember, you have to slow down, stop, refill, pay, restart, and rejoin the road each time – even one extra fill-up can cancel out the saving made by speeding.

To get the most from your motoring, never go faster than is absolutely necessary; never slow or accelerate sharply if it can be avoided; always take your opportunities; *never* take chances!

## My car will do the ton

Not legally it won't, unless you happen to be driving it on a closed track or on a German autobahn. Don't ever let yourself be needled into competitive driving by somebody else's idle boasts. It'll only be a matter of time before, if you do that, you lose either your licence or your life.

However, many drivers don't know what their true speed is at any time, because they have never checked their speedos. If you wish to drive accurately, it's something you can do for yourself.

What's more, it's well worth doing, because normal car speedometers are almost invariably inaccurate. During 1986/87 a motoring magazine notable for the accuracy of its tests reported on 35 different cars. Only one of them had a speedo that was completely free of error! At a true speed of 30mph, speedometer readings varied from 29mph to 34mph. At 40mph, the range was from 39mph to 44mph. At a true 50mph, readings varied from 48mph to 56mph. A true 60mph produced speedo indications from 57mph to 67mph. And at 70mph, the results varied from a pessimistic 66mph to a wildly optimistic 78mph. On average, the speedos read fast – by 2 mph at 30, 40 and 50; by 3 mph at 60; and by nearly 4 mph at 70. Two speedometers underestimated speed throughout the range – one was showing only 66mph when the true speed was 70mph –

and the degree of error on two of them was enough to make them illegal. At an indicated 100mph, incidentally, the worst of the speedos would have been over-estimating the car's true speed by over 11mph – but then, 'My car will do 88.6mph' perhaps doesn't have quite the same ring to it!

It's a fairly straightforward job to get a reasonably accurate check on a speedo, providing you have a watch with a digital stopwatch facility and a reliable friend to operate it. You also need a reasonably quiet stretch of motorway and a notebook and pencil.

Motorways are marked at 100m intervals along the far edge of the hard shoulder. Select a straight and level stretch of the inner lane that is clear for at least a mile ahead and behind, and set up a 70mph cruise on your speedometer. Tell your watch operator to choose a marker ahead of you and to start his watch just as it is blotted out by the car's nearside windscreen pillar. He should then call out 'One– two– three–' as succeeding posts are passed, and as the fourth passes out of view behind the pillar he should stop the watch. Providing you have kept the needle steady on 70mph, you should now have the time it has taken you to cover 400m.

Repeat the exercise at 60mph and, if possible, at 50mph too. You can then clear the motorway – it's not advisable to drop down to speeds as low as 30 or 40mph – and work out the error. That's simple enough: just divide 900 by the time in seconds, and there's your speed in miles per hour. Apply the appropriate correction when you're driving – for example, if the stopwatch gave 13.4 seconds for 400m, your speed was a smidgeon over 67mph. Therefore, your speedometer over-reads by 3mph, and to compensate for that you should drive at an indicated 73mph to achieve a genuine 70mph cruise.

As a rule of thumb, speedometer error at 30mph and 40mph is likely to be virtually the same as the error at 50mph, so the 50mph figure can safely be applied lower down the scale.

While you're using the motorway you could also check the accuracy of your trip meter. This has to be done over a run of 10 miles, using the markers. Have your passenger sitting ready with his notebook, watching the kilometre readings on the posts. It's easiest to start the check on a round number – 10.0, 20.0, 30.0 and so forth. As you approach the chosen marker, he should ask you to call out your tripmeter reading, so he can note it down. He then settles down to wait for the marker 16.1 kilometres further up the road – say, the post marked 46.1. As you pass it, call out the new trip reading. The difference between the two should be precisely 10 miles. If it is more, the odd decimals multiplied by 10 will indicate the percentage by which the meter is over-reading. If it is less, the amount by which it falls short of 10 miles is multiplied by 10 to give the percentage under-read.

It may not seem to be a safety factor to know how accurate your tripmeter is, but it can be valuable. Under bad conditions, you can use a trip reading to help establish how far you still have to go to a tricky turn-off, for instance. It will also enable you to calculate an accurate fuel consumption, and could make all the difference between reaching the next motorway service area with fuel in hand, or finding yourself stranded five miles down the road, with all the attendant dangers and inconvenience.

Accurate driving demands accurate information – and you can't have too much of that.

# Now You Can Really Start Learning

Your full driving licence, new and unsullied, is tucked safely away in pocket or handbag. Right – you are no longer a novice, but remember that you are still a learner, and that you will be for thousands of miles to come. You know the rudiments of driving, and you have passed an elementary test of competence to drive unsupervised. All the major lessons, however, are still to be learned, and only time and experience will teach them.

Of course, you can help the process along by taking advanced tuition. There is almost certainly a driving school not far from your home that can offer a suitable course, and it's unlikely to set you back more than the cost of a pint of beer each day for a year.

In some parts of the country, too, there are skid pans on which you can learn proper car control on ice-rink surfaces. And there are specialist courses combining track and roadwork to teach safe high-speed driving. *Safe* is the operative word: any fool can drive a car fast – till the accident happens.

Meantime, we'll take a brief look at some of the situations the driving test *didn't* test . . .

## Open-road corners

So far, we've only considered the type of corner likely to be encountered in the test itself: mainly urban, mainly restricted to a maximum of 40mph. Your first long drive will rapidly convince you that they were not typical.

For a start, outside towns the bends you encounter will be on

60mph limit roads, and the traffic stream will be moving at – or, human nature being what it is, above – that speed. At the least, you need to know the basic technique for faster cornering and how to establish a 'line' through the bend that does not involve following the kerb at a constant 1m clearance. The accompanying figures show how left-hand and right-hand bends can be tackled briskly and safely.

The first requirements are to start in the right position on the road, with the car travelling at the right speed, and with the right gear selected. For a left-hand bend you need as early a sight through the bend as possible, since anything from a file of pedestrians to a broken-down lorry could be lurking close to the verge in the area that you can't see from a kerb-hugging approach. Against that you have to balance the danger from oncoming traffic, for if you lose control your car will tend to go straight on into the opposite carriageway.

So on the approach move out to a position no closer to the centreline than 18/24 in. Do all your braking and selection of a lower gear on this straight run-in, so that you arrive at the start of the corner all ready to turn. From this vantage point, towards the road centre, you get the best possible view into the bend. Turn in smoothly, and keep the speed constant – if possible, neither accelerate nor brake until the car is again running straight. At the apex of the bend, tighten the turn to bring the car down the camber, aiming to be 1m from the verge when you hit the straight again. As you begin to exit from the bend, apply power, joining the straight at your chosen cruising speed.

'In slow, out fast,' is the formula for quick but safe cornering. 'In fast, out feet first' is the ironic comment racing drivers often add!

A right-hand bend demands a different technique. To get the best possible view, you need to start the approach from the normal position 1m from the kerb. Again, all slowing and gear selection is done with the car straight, so that when you reach the bend itself all you have to do is steer!

Keep the car to the left as you turn into the bend – you need to be as far away as possible from approaching traffic that may overcook the bend and plough on across the centre-line; and you still need to see as far round the curve as you can. At the apex, start to ease the car up the camber towards the centre-line so that, as the straight opens up before you, power can be applied to accelerate away on a line 18/24in from the crown. Then gradually move back to the left-hand side.

What's the correct speed for a bend? One that allows the car to go through in a smooth sweep, without tyre squeal, without deviating either at front or rear, without endangering either its driver or other road users. On corners, as on straights, the speed must be low enough to ensure that the car can be stopped within the distance the driver can see to be clear. Bends can be very unforgiving and to be just a little too fast can be fatal. Asked to define a dangerous speed, Stirling Moss replied 'Thirty-five miles per hour in a thirty-mile-per-hour bend is a highly dangerous speed.' He was right!

## Motorway driving

Motorways are the safest roads in the country – which perhaps says more about the rest of Britain's road network than about the motorways themselves. From the driver's seat, on your first M-way excursion, you will certainly find it hard to believe. Rep-mobiles blast past you at anything up to 20mph above the 70mph speed limit; drivers of sporting saloons give vehicles ahead of them anything but a sporting chance by sitting feet behind in the overtaking lane impatiently flashing a battery of halogen headlamps, and in the inner lanes those latter-day lemmings, the drivers of heavy goods vehicles, contribute to motorway madness by driving, perhaps three or four together, nose to tail with not half a car's length between them and with all but the leading driver totally unsighted.

Perhaps the trouble is that in good conditions a motorway is just too reassuring. Compared with normal roads it has wide open spaces. It is reasonably straight, and you could see ahead for miles if it weren't for the traffic in between. After a while you adjust mentally and a sustained 70mph cruise looks from the wheel no faster than a 30mph dawdle elsewhere.

Don't be fooled by appearances. Once on the motorway you are in a hostile environment, and driving there requires more concentration – not less.

As a first step, disabuse yourself of the idea that a three-lane motorway contains a slow lane, a middle lane, and a fast lane. It doesn't. It comprises a left-hand lane in which you should normally drive, plus two overtaking lanes that you should enter *only* for overtaking, returning to the left-hand lane as soon as you can do so with safety. So, if joining a motorway at its start, begin in the left-hand lane and move out only if there is slower traffic ahead.

You'll have to remember that traffic from behind will – speed limit or no speed limit – be closing on you much faster than usual. Don't rely on just one look in the mirrors before signalling and moving into the next lane to your right. Look forward again, then switch your eyes back to the mirror so that you can judge just how quickly the traffic behind is gaining ground. If it's still far enough away to make overtaking safe, signal and change lanes quickly. Then cancel the signal, so following drivers will know that you do not intend to move into the outer overtaking lane.

You may be joining the motorway at a junction. If so, you will enter by way of a slip road which subsequently becomes an acceleration lane. As you approach the point at which the slip road merges with the motorway, look back down the M-way to your right – *well back*. If there is a safe gap, accelerate to 70mph along the acceleration lane, signalling a right turn, and join the left-hand lane smoothly. If you misjudged the speed of approaching traffic, slow or even stop in the acceleration lane until you can be sure that it's safe to enter the motorway itself. *Never* try to out-accelerate traffic that's already moving at 70mph.

Lane discipline is essential. Don't weave from one lane to another. If you have moved into the middle overtaking lane to pass slower traffic and there is another line of slower vehicles in the left-hand lane a hundred yards or so further ahead you should maintain position until you overtake them too. *Then* move back. The same applies to the outer overtaking lane, with the proviso that you should have a reasonable speed differential. There's no point sitting there and crawling past at a relative speed that's no more than walking pace. You should have slowed, instead, to match speeds and waited for traffic to thin out – as it will.

Separation is equally important. Leave too much space between yourself and the vehicle ahead, rather than too little. It's particularly important to hold well back when coming up behind a lorry. For a start, it will completely block your forward vision. For another, it is likely that if it has to make an emergency stop it may outbrake you. Impossible? Not so. For example, you are travelling at 70mph and closing on a lorry that's cruising at 60mph when you see its brake lights come on. That means the driver is *already* braking. From 60mph, a lorry with brakes of average efficiency will come to a dead stop in 285ft (87m). It will take you a split second to realise that this is no mere flash of the brake lights, but for real. Then you react – total time, one second – and also brake. But you are braking from 70mph, not 60mph, and though your brakes are more efficient you have closed in by a further 100 feet (30m), so *your* total stopping distance from the point at which you saw the lorry's brake lights will be at least 300 ft (91m). Which means that you could come to rest, in theory, 15ft inside the lorry – in practice, crumpled into the back of it.

Most motorway accidents are 'shunts', made particularly deadly because other following vehicles have less and less time in which to avoid the mess ahead, and a multiple pile-up results. The Highway Code's rule of thumb for separation – one metre per mile per hour of speed – may sound hopelessly impractical but it's sound thinking. If you allow a minimum separation of the distance between the motorway markers between the front of your car and the vehicle in front at 70mph you will have time and space in which to act in an emergency.

Be particularly careful when leaving the motorway. Get into the left-hand lane early – even if it means following a 50mph mobile traffic jam, it'll cost you only a few seconds on your overall journey time – and signal a left turn as you reach the 300-yard marker. Turn off up the slip road, and use its length to slow down to normal road speeds. If you keep 70mph on the clock, you may find yourself taking a short cut right across the succeeding roundabout, brakes locked and tyres smoking!

There's always a possibility that you may not reach that turn-off point. Motorways are hard on cars, and breakdowns are not infrequent. That's another good reason for using the left-hand lane as much as possible, since it's easy enough to coast from there straight on to the hard shoulder, signalling a left turn as you do so. The same mechanical failure in either of the overtaking lanes makes it harder to gain the comparative safety of the hard shoulder – hazardous, in the case of the outermost overtaking lane, with two lanes of traffic to cross with, perhaps, no means of propulsion.

If you're really caught in the outermost lane, with no hope of reaching the hard shoulder, mentally damn the letter of the law and immediately switch on your hazard warning flashers, pumping the brake pedal just enough to flash your stoplamps too. Flashing lights catch the eye more easily than static ones, and you need every split second you can get. With following traffic warned that something is wrong, you may still be able to reach the hard shoulder. Remember, though, that some fool scorching up the outer overtaking lane is quite likely to try to dive through on your left instead of stopping. If the traffic is really thick – in more ways than one! – keep the lights flashing, pull up close to the fence, and pray for a police car. Unless the motorway is unusually quiet it's probably better to stay with the car than to attempt to abandon it, but that's a matter for individual judgement.

Where you have managed to reach the hard shoulder, coast as close as you can to an emergency telephone (or stop as soon as you can, if you've just passed one) and make sure the car is as far to the left on the hard shoulder as possible. Leave it through the passenger door, and under no circumstances walk or stand between the car and passing traffic. Any passengers should leave the car, and scramble up on to the verge – many broken-down cars have been hit by other vehicles while standing on the hard shoulder – and, hard-hearted though it may seem, leave any animals shut up inside it. Don't try to fiddle with the car yourself, ace though you may be at doing-it-yourself. This car is in a dangerous place, so leave the rescue operation to professionals who're paid to take the risks. Walk to the emergency phone – keeping as far from the traffic as you can – and call for help. Then go and join your passengers up on the verge. Don't be tempted to get back into the car, come rain, hail or snow. Conditions like that make the danger greater, not less. Help won't be long delayed, and you'll be able to leave in the safety of the breakdown vehicle.

## Night driving

Some drivers actually prefer to make journeys at night, believing that anticipation is easier when the course of roads is traced out by the pattern of headlamp beams. Others abhor it. Either way, eventually you'll have to do it, if only because Britain has dark winters.

Obviously, the first requirement is that you should be able to see where you're going, so your car's lights must be in good order and properly adjusted. If your car is past its youth, the likelihood is that the headlamp reflectors will no longer be as efficient as they could be. Inspect them for signs of tarnishing. They should be a bright silver. If not, have a new set fitted – they're usually surprisingly cheap. In any case, get a garage to set them up properly. Their beam-setting equipment allows this to be done accurately.

Make sure the lenses are clean before each trip, and that your windscreen isn't partly obscured by dirt, inside or out.

If you are travelling on roads where your car will be subjected to spray from other vehicles, and your trip is one of more than 40 miles, it pays to stop briefly at round the mid-way point and clean the headlamp lenses again. They can accumulate a surprising deposit of road filth in 20 miles – quite enough to reduce your illumination seriously.

Much of a night-time journey will be spent on dipped beams, which also cut the distance you can see ahead. Your speed must be lowered accordingly. There's little future in speeding into the blackness and *hoping* that the road is clear. Absence of lights does not indicate absence of obstructions, and darkness can cloak a broken-down tractor or an Indian file of pedestrians.

You cannot assume, either, that there is no danger on a motor-way. Lorries shed large blocks of wood, or tyre treads – even, on occasion, a whole spare wheel. Hitting any such obstruction can damage your car and put you out of control.

Dip early for approaching vehicles, and don't be tempted to look towards their lights. Concentrate on the left-hand side of your own carriageway, looking down your own dipped beams. Occasionally you may be blinded because an approaching driver has either badly-set lamps or has failed to dip – an easy mistake to make. If that happens, slow down and don't switch to main beam until the offending car is at least alongside you. One blinded driver is bad enough: two could be a disaster.

Remember to use the dipping facility on your interior mirror as following traffic approaches closely enough for their lights to become bothersome – some experienced motorists actually like to leave a film of dirt on the rear screen to minimise dazzle from the rear – and when you yourself come up behind another vehicle dip early to make life easier for its driver. Keep far enough back to ensure that your lights don't hit his mirrors – safer for you, too, if he should stop without warning.

In town, remember that dipped headlamps must be used at all times – parking lights are for parking only. Street lamps may help by providing even illumination, but in side streets it may be patchy, and pedestrians may lurk in the shadows between the pools of light. Even in reasonably well-lit areas, a pedestrian in dark clothing is all too easily 'lost' against the dark road surface, so exercise particular care in built-up areas.

# Bad weather driving

If you think that bad-weather motoring consists mainly of dealing with ice and snow, you're wrong. Mainly, it's rain that's the hazard: and a pretty deadly one at that.

Heavy rain in itself is a danger, since it can cut vision to virtually nothing almost without warning. Once the wipers are so inundated by water that they can no longer clear it from the screen, the screen might just as well be opaque. When driving in squally showers, therefore, you must be prepared to slow down if you can see rain actually ricochetting off the road ahead. Use the fastest wiper speeds, too.

Rain means surface water, which can lead to another danger – aquaplaning. This occurs when the tyres are unable to clear away all the water from the footprint areas. The surface film then effectively interposes between the tyre and the ground so that the car is actually riding on water. Both steering and braking control can be lost – usually at speeds above 50/60mph. All the driver can do is ease off, without braking, and give the tyres a chance to bite again. Make sure that the steering is kept straight ahead, though; the moment grip is regained the car will swerve, if the front wheels are deflected one way or the other.

Avoid driving through deep puddles – especially, at speed and with just one wheel. The effect is to cause a sudden deceleration on that side of the car, which can be violent enough to wrench the steering hard over. Even with two hands on the wheel it's hard enough to retain control. Driving one-handed – perhaps operating a minor control, or trying to switch channels on the car radio – you would find it almost impossible to avoid driving into the verge. On a tarmac road, at night, even large puddles are very hard to see – they simply merge into the blackness of the night and the road – so especial care has to be taken at night in heavy rain, particularly if you need to move left to avoid oncoming traffic.

Light rain can be just as tricky – it makes the surface greasy, encouraging skidding. It also has the same effect on the windscreen, the wipers simply skating over an emulsion of oily road dirt and water. Frequent use of screenwashers and wipers will help to prevent it.

High winds are a particular danger on exposed roads – motorways in particular. Anticipate a strong crosswind hitting the car without warning as you emerge from the shelter of such windbreaks as houses, wooded areas, or hedgerows, and be ready to apply steering correction. It pays to keep a constant eye on wind direction, so that you can compensate immediately if any swerve starts to develop.

On motorways the effects of side winds are often felt just as you overtake a high-sided vehicle. The sudden blast as you emerge from its shelter can throw your car right across a motorway lane.

Ice is the motorist's most implacable enemy – especially black ice, whose presence can often not be seen even when the car is actually on it, though it can be sensed by a sudden cessation of tyre noise. Braking, sudden deceleration, or coarse deflection of the steering wheel can all send the car into a skid. The best course, as with all skidding, is to declutch immediately, leave the brakes alone, and concentrate on skid correction by steering into the skid, then centring the wheel as the car straightens. The worst possible action is to brake. If you do, the wheels will lock – and locked wheels won't steer.

On ice or snow drive in the highest possible gear that will still give control – lifting off the throttle in too low a gear has the same effect as braking. Snow itself is not particularly hazardous unless it is deep enough to force the car to stop and stick. Under blizzard conditions, motorists have died from exposure after abandoning a snow-bound car only a quarter of a mile from habitations. If caught in such a trap, stay with the car. Go outside at intervals, well wrapped up – use the car's carpets as a cloak, if necessary – long enough to dig away all snow from around the exhaust pipe. You will then be able to run the engine for a few minutes at a time to warm up the interior through the heater. Without a clear exhaust, there's always a danger of carbon monoxide poisoning.

Usually, snow will be only inches thick and the tyres will bite through, giving reasonable control. Keep in a high gear, brake only gently – and then only when necessary – and restrict steering deflection. Where other traffic has cut ruts, stay in them. They make it easier to keep going, even though you may have to work hard to get out again.

If snow does bring you to a standstill, you may still be able to reverse out along your own wheeltracks. If wheelspin develops, try inserting car mats under both driving wheels – at the front if you want to go forward; behind the wheel for reversing. If you get moving, keep moving till you reach hard road, then go back for your mats on foot. An off-road trick that sometimes works is to switch off the engine, engage gear (first or reverse) and, leaving the clutch home, turn the ignition key. The car may then move off slowly, driven by the starter motor, before the engine restarts and, if all goes well, brings you clear.


## Talk yourself through

Talking to yourself, they say, is the first sign of madness. It can also be the first sign of an advanced driver in the making, since giving a running commentary on your progress is a good way of maintaining concentration and really making you *think* about your driving. The police use the method in training – and nobody has higher standards.

A typical commentary might be:-

'I am driving down a residential road subject to a 30mph speed limit. I am in third gear, at the limit. Left, 200 yards ahead, there's a car standing in a driveway, rather close to the road, so I'll back off a little in case it emerges without warning. Yes, I can see it moving. The driver can't see me yet because his vision's restricted by a hedge. I'd better be prepared to pull up. Yes – there he goes; straight out and turning left and doesn't even know I'm here. Hold back to give adequate separation, and watch to see if he does anything else daft. He has. He's accelerated over the limit and now he's drawing away, so I return to 30mph.

'Traffic sign ahead – triangular, so it's a warning of some kind. Yes, crossing point for elderly people – slow down and be prepared to give way. Elderly man near the sign – may want to cross, and he could be part-blind or deaf. Keep watching. No, he's walking on. Pass the sign. Back to 30mph.

'I can see shadows between the third and fourth cars in that line parked on the right, 100 yards ahead. Check mirrors – clear behind – and ready to brake if nec . . . . Hell! Off accelerator, firm push on the brake, declutch. I'm at a standstill and two kids are lucky to be alive . . . '

Carried out as a regular exercise, the running commentary really makes your driving stick in your mind, highlighting not just other people's mistakes but, more importantly, your own.

But if you have still to pass your test, *don't* try it on the examiner!

# The Highway Code-
# Questions & Answers

# The Highway Code

The Highway Code gives invaluable information and guidance for everyone who uses the roads, whether as a driver, a cyclist, a pedestrian or a horse rider. Yet, for many of us, it is a necessary part of studying for the driving test and nothing more. Once the test is over, we never open it again.

This section of the book is for those who want to pass the test — and for those who have been driving for years. Do you know how to tell when you are in a 30 mph zone, even when there are no signs? Do you know how you could tell a STOP sign from a Give Way sign, even if it was covered in snow? The answers to those questions and hundreds more, on every aspect of highway behaviour from negotiating roundabouts to parking restrictions, from a breakdown on a level crossing to coping with accident victims are to be found here.

The questions are divided into sections, so that you can test your knowledge on each aspect of roadcraft separately. Needless to say they often overlap and you will find that an answer from one section crops up as a question in another. Tackling the same rule from a different standpoint is a useful aid to understanding, and full understanding of the contents of the Highway Code will result in better driving techniques, more consideration for other road users and safer motoring.

# Signs and Markings

**1** What shape are most road signs giving orders?

**2** When these signs are prohibitive, what colour is their border?

**3** How do you identify a bus lane?

**4** How can you tell the parking distance from a zebra crossing?

**5** What is the difference between restrictions indicated by yellow lines painted on the kerb and yellow lines painted along the edge of the carriageway?

**6** What type of level crossing is indicated by
   a.   A triangular sign with the silhouette of a gate.
   b.   A triangular sign with the silhouette of a train.

**7** What background colour would you expect to find on motorway signs?

**8** What colour signs do you expect to find on a primary road?

**9** What is the meaning of the following signs?

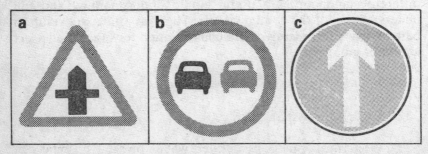

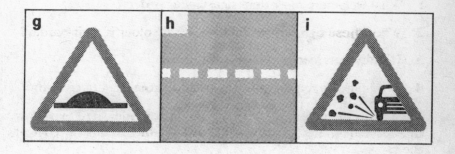

**10**   What is the nature of triangular signs?

**11**   What is the meaning of a circular sign with a red border and two diagonal red lines crossed on a blue background?

**12**   Describe a hospital sign.

**13**   What must you do, as a driver, when you see a hospital sign?

**14** What do the following signs tell you?

**15** The road signs indicating temporary lane closure and those indicating permanent reduction of lanes ahead both have arrows pointing ahead and a T-shaped motif. Describe the difference between these signs.

**16** Name three warning signs which have black silhouettes of animals.

**17** What restrictions are indicated by
   a.   A single yellow line at the edge of the carriageway.
   b.   A double yellow line at the edge of the carriageway.

**18** Describe the difference between a white line on the road telling you to stop at a STOP sign and the white line painted on the road where you must stop at traffic signals.

**19** You are driving on a country road with white dashes down the centre. When these dashes lengthen, what does it mean?

**20** You are travelling on the motorway, obeying a 50 mph speed limit which has been in force for some time, because of road works taking place on the nearside lane. Once you have cleared the road works and the restriction is at an end, what sign would you expect to see?

**21** What does a sign showing a white R on a green background signify?

**22** What is the difference between the sign with a white R on a green background and a sign with a black R on a white background?

**23** What is the purpose of arrows painted on the road at the approach to traffic lights?

**24** You are travelling along a road with double white lines down the centre. The line nearer to you is solid, indicating that you should not cross it. Name three occasions when it would be permissible to cross this line.

**25** What is the meaning of a circular sign with a red border and a silhouette of a man walking?

**26** Name two places where you might find a box junction.

**27** The lorry travelling ahead of you is displaying a yellow warning triangle. What is it carrying?

**28** You see triple yellow chevrons marked on the kerb. What does this mean and what additional sign would you expect to find?

**29** Name the various ways that might mark a one-way street.

**30** A rectangular sign pictures red, amber and green lights with a diagonal stripe across them. What does this indicate?

**31** How do you identify a bus stop?

**32** There are double white lines down the centre of the road but the line nearer to you is broken. What does this mean?

**33** You see a triangular sign with the silhouette of an aeroplane. What is this telling you?

**34** You see KEEP CLEAR painted on the road in large letters. What is it telling you to keep clear?

**35** Describe the sign that means parking is restricted to permit holders only.

**36** What does a brown directional road sign indicate?

**37** You see a blue direction sign with a white silhouette of a man walking, pointing the way to the public library. What does this tell you, as a motorist?

**38** You are going on holiday by road and looking for a special holiday route. What sign should you look for?

**39** On a level crossing with three signs, one above the other, the top sign shows two black humps on a white background, inside a red-edged triangle. What does it mean?

**40** Study the road signs below and answer the following questions about them:

a. This sign, with broken white lines marked across the carriageway, means that you must stop before turning into a major road, whether there is traffic approaching or not. TRUE or FALSE?

b. You will be meeting two-way traffic ahead. TRUE or FALSE?

c. This sign, with white arrows on a blue background, warns of a mini-roundabout ahead. TRUE or FALSE?

d. This sign indicates that children may be going to or from school. TRUE or FALSE?

e. There is a road junction ahead, so you should give way. TRUE or FALSE?

f. This sign, with a large white arrow pointed ahead and a small red arrow pointing towards you, on a blue background, means that you have priority over vehicles coming from the opposite direction. TRUE or FALSE?

g.  This sign shows a black, curved arrow with a red diagonal line through the middle and means No Right Turn. TRUE or FALSE?
h.  Motor vehicles prohibited. TRUE or FALSE?
i.  This blue sign with a white 30 tells you the maximum speed that is allowed on the road. TRUE or FALSE?
j.  The motif on this warning triangle means that a side road is about to join the main road. TRUE or FALSE?
k.  Two way traffic crosses a one-way road. TRUE or FALSE?
l.  This road marking, with long markings and short gaps, down the middle of the road, means that you should only overtake if you are turning right. TRUE or FALSE?

**41**  Give the meaning of the following three cycle signs:
a.  A black cycle within a red circle.
b.  A white cycle on a blue background.
c.  A black cycle in a red triangle.

**42**  You see a red triangle containing the silhouette of an adult and child walking. Does this mean

126

a. Pedestrian crossing ahead.
b. Pedestrians walking in the road ahead.
c. School exit.
d. Controlled school crossing.

**43** A rectangular blue sign shows a T shape; the vertical shaft of the T is white, its crossbar is red. Does this mean
a. A T junction.
b. No through road.
c. No entry.

**44** A circular blue sign shows with a bicycle on the left and an adult with a child walking on the right. Does this mean
a. Pedestrians and cyclists prohibited.
b. Beware of pedestrians and cyclists.
c. A route for both pedestrians and cyclists.

**45** How many yellow lines would you expect to find painted over the kerb when the nearby time plate says **No Loading Mon-Fri 8.00-9.30 a.m., 4.30-6.30 p.m.** Is it
a. One.
b. Two.
c. Three.

**46** A white triangle painted on the road has a thick base and the point facing towards you. Does this mean
a. No parking.
b. You should prepare to get in lane.
c. Warning that you must give way ahead.

**47** Describe the sign that warns of overhead electric cables.

*Answers on page 192.*

# Driving Conditions and Hazards

**1** If you are in charge of a heavy vehicle in poor conditions, when it is wet or misty, what must you bear in mind?

**2** When driving in fog, what is your main concern, for the sake of safety?

**3** It is a wet day and every vehicle that passes throws up spray and dirt. When you stop for petrol what should you take the opportunity to check?

**4** What special difficulty would you find when leaving the motorway in fog?

**5** Before setting out on a night drive, what should you be sure to check?

**6** The road is wet and slippery, which means that it will take you longer to pull up in case of emergency. By how much should you increase the gap between your car and the car in front?

**7** White chevrons on a long, horizontal black sign point to the left. What does this tell you about the road ahead?

**8** When you see a skull and crossbones on a white diamond on the back of a lorry, what does this mean?

**9**  Describe the motorway signal which means that you must proceed no further in a particular lane.

**10**  What special difficulties should you bear in mind when overtaking at dusk?

**11**  You are negotiating a roundabout at the same time as a long vehicle. What problems is this likely to present?

**12**  What action should you take if you are dazzled by approaching headlights?

**13**  Your vehicle breaks down on the highway at night. You know there is a garage a short distance ahead. Is it better to push the car off the highway and leave it there while you contact the garage or to push it as far as the garage?

**14**  What warning is given of an approaching train at an automatic half barrier level crossing?

**15**  A level crossing without barriers shows a diagonal white cross with red borders. How does the sign tell you whether the crossing is used by one or two railway lines?

**16**  Which triangular warning sign contains three arrows?

**17**  Name four places where parking might interfere with emergency services.

**18**  How can you best avoid rear-end collisions on motorways?

**19**  You are approaching a level crossing in a nose-to-tail traffic queue. What precautions should you take?

**20**  What should you do when you are passing animals on the highway?

**21**  What should you *not* do as you pass animals?

**22**  You are driving past a line of parked vehicles. How much clearance do you allow for safety?

**23** You see an ice cream van parked in a suburban street. What should you do?

**24** What particular precautions should you take if there is a bus lane on your left and you are turning into a street on the left?

**25** The fog that has surrounded you for the past half hour seems to be lifting and at last you can see the road ahead. Breathing a sigh of relief you start to accelerate. What should you bear in mind?

**26** You are driving in fog and you can see the tail lights of a car ahead. Your safest course is to tuck in behind and adjust your speed to follow the vehicle in front. TRUE or FALSE?

**27** You should never drive close behind another vehicle with your headlights full on. TRUE or FALSE?

**28** While you are driving carefully in the fog, another car comes up behind you, hanging onto your tail lights. The safest course is to speed up so that you leave him behind. TRUE or FALSE?

**29** As you draw up at a pedestrian crossing you should signal to the pedestrians that it is now safe to cross the road. TRUE or FALSE?

**30** You should treat a pelican crossing with a central refuge as two separate crossings. TRUE or FALSE?

**31** When there is no pavement pedestrians walk on the right facing the traffic but a procession or marching scout troop would walk on the left. TRUE or FALSE?

**32** You wait at a level crossing while a train passes but the lights still flash and the barrier stays down. If this continues for more than three minutes with no train arriving you should use the telephone at the crossing to contact the signalman. TRUE or FALSE?

**33** You find that tinted spectacles help in daytime driving by reducing glare. They are also a good idea at night to prevent being dazzled by the lights of approaching cars. TRUE or FALSE?

**34** You are driving in a busy city street which has a specially designated bus lane. You want to turn left but are held up by a line of traffic waiting to go straight on. You are allowed to use the bus lane to bypass the line of stationary traffic. TRUE or FALSE?

**35** You are driving along the high street when you see the amber light flashing on a pelican crossing. This means you should
    a.   Give way to pedestrians already on the crossing.
    b.   Give way to pedestrians about to use the crossing.
    c.   You have the right of way.

**36** You are driving a car without fog lamps on a foggy day. What lights should you use?
    a.   Side lights.
    b.   Dipped headlights.
    c.   Full headlights.

**37** When driving in fog, it is important to keep a safe distance behind the vehicle in front. Is this distance
    a.   Two car lengths.
    b.   Three car lengths.
    c.   So that you can pull up well within the distance you can see ahead.

**38** You are driving out of a hotel car park; the exit crosses a footpath to reach the road. The road is clear of traffic but a pedestrian is approaching on the footpath. In this situation should you
    a.   Give way to the pedestrian.
    b.   Expect the pedestrian to give way to you.

**39** You should not let your vehicle stand near a junction, as this could make it difficult for others drivers to see properly. What minimum space should you leave? Is it
    a.   10 metres (33 ft).
    b.   15 metres (49 ft).
    c.   20 metres (66 ft).

**40** In which of these situations should you use your hazard warning lights?
    a.   When your vehicle has broken down.

b.   While you are loading or unloading.
c.   While you make a brief stop in a no parking area.
d.   While being towed by another vehicle.

**41**   A triangular sign warns you that you may find farm animals in the road. What is shown in the triangle? Is it
a.   An exclamation mark.
b.   The silhouette of a cow.
c.   The silhouette of a horse.

**42**   Outside your child's school, you find the words 'School Keep Clear' written in yellow on the road across the gateway. On either side of these words are yellow zigzags. Does this mean that you can wait on the zigzag area
a.   Any time, so long as you are well clear of the exit itself.
b.   Only while you are picking up or setting down children.
c.   Never.

**43**   You are travelling downhill on a narrow country road when you see a car coming uphill towards you. There is not sufficient room to pass so one of you will have to draw into the side of the road. Do you
a.   Give priority to the other car.
b.   Expect the other driver to give you priority.

**44**   The white line down the middle of the road has long markings with short gaps. Does this mean
a.   You must only cross the line when passing stationary vehicles or turning left.
b.   You must take extra care in crossing and do so only when you can see that the road well ahead is clear.

**45**   Pedestrians walking on the road at night can cut the risks of accidents by wearing reflective material. Reflective material can be picked up by headlights up to
a.   Twice as far as ordinary clothes.
b.   Three times as far as ordinary clothes.
c.   Four times as far as ordinary clothes.

*Answers on page 197.*

# Junctions and Roundabouts

**1**  What is a box junction?

**2**  A green direction sign indicates that you are approaching a roundabout ahead and have a choice of four destinations. How many entrances/exits has the roundabout?

**3**  You are approaching a large town on a major route and want to avoid the busy centre by taking the ring road. What sign should you look for?

**4**  What should you do as you approach a crossroads with no signs?

**5**  What should you always bear in mind as you approach a junction road?

**6**  What special problems do long vehicles present at junctions?

**7**  You want to reach a town on the right-hand side of the motor-way. Which side do you exit?

**8**  You are approaching a junction on a three-lane section of a primary road. The traffic lights are green and so is the filter arrow indicating a turn to the left. Which lane do you take if you are going straight on?

**9**  What is the purpose of a roundabout?

**10**  What sign indicates that there is a roundabout ahead?

**11**  What is a mini-roundabout?

**12** Study the following diagrams. Which indicates the correct position for a car turning left from a side road into a main road?

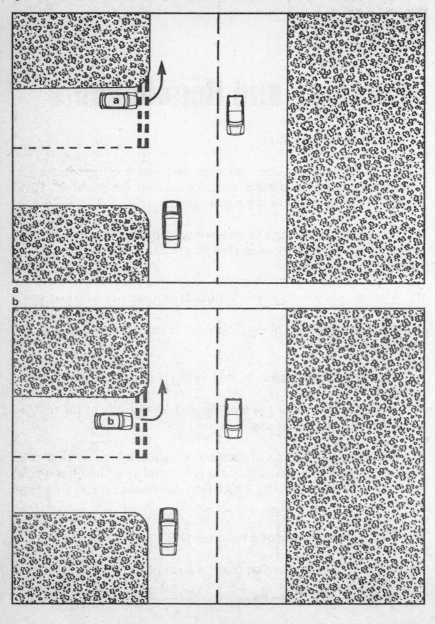

a

b

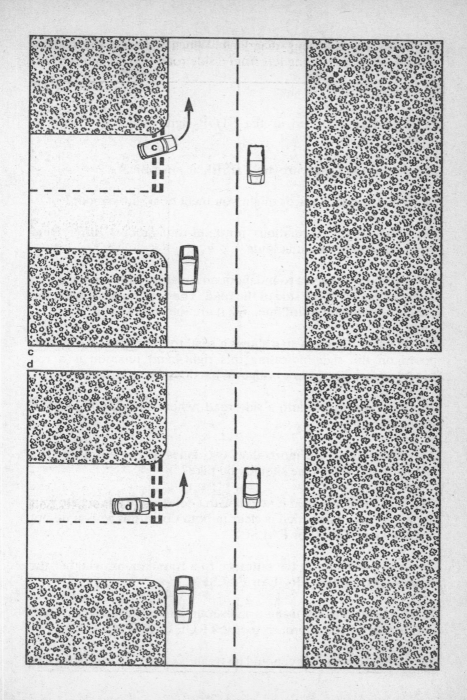

**13** Where would you expect to find indications about junctions ahead?

**14** Describe a STOP sign.

**15** You have stopped at the STOP sign. When is it safe to proceed?

**16** Which road users are most at risk at junctions?

**17** What special hazards might you meet on a roundabout?

**18** How do the regulations for mini-roundabouts differ from those on ordinary roundabouts?

**19** As you approach a roundabout on a major road, you see green backed markers at the side of the road. The first has three bars, the second two and the third one. What are they telling you?

**20** A white direction sign shows a road to the right but superimposed on the sign indicating this right-hand junction is a red triangle, warning of a low bridge. What does the red triangle show?

**21** As you turn left into a side road, where should you position your vehicle?

**22** When there are more than two lanes at the entrance to a roundabout, which lane should you take?

**23** You come to a road junction with a solid white line across your approach. The main road is clear in both directions so you do not need to stop. TRUE or FALSE?

**24** You must stop at the entrance to a roundabout, whether the road is clear or not. TRUE or FALSE?

**25** Vehicles already using a mini-roundabout have right of way over traffic on the approach roads. TRUE or FALSE?

**26** A dual carriageway should be treated as two separate roads, so that you pause in the central reservation until it is safe to join the second half of the road. TRUE or FALSE?

**27**   When you plan to go straight on at a roundabout, you use no signal on approach. TRUE or FALSE?

**28**   At a junction normally controlled by traffic lights, a policeman is controlling the exceptionally heavy traffic. He has his back to you and his arm is extended in STOP sign but the green filter light is showing on the traffic lights so you are allowed to turn left. TRUE or FALSE?

**29**   Local direction signs have white backgrounds. What colour are the borders? Is it
   a.   Black.
   b.   Blue.
   c.   Green.
   d.   Yellow.

**30**   You are turning right at a junction and a car approaching from the other direction is also turning right. How should you normally pass? Is it
   a.   Nearside to nearside.
   b.   Offside to offside.
   c.   Whichever is more convenient.

**31**   You are approaching a roundabout with three exits and you intend to turn right. Do you
   a.   Use the right indicator on approach, maintain this signal while on the roundabout then change to left as you pass the second exit.
   b.   Use no signal on approach, signal right as you pass the first exit, then left as you pass the second.
   c.   Use no signal until you pass the second exit, then use the left indicator.

**32**   Under what circumstances do you use the right-hand lane on a roundabout? Is it
   a.   If you are turning right.
   b.   If you are turning left.

c.  If you are going straight on and the left hand lane is blocked.
d.  Only when overtaking.

**33** Study the following diagrams, showing traffic crossing a box junction. Cars A and B are driving straight on; cars C and D are turning right. Which of these drivers is behaving correctly?

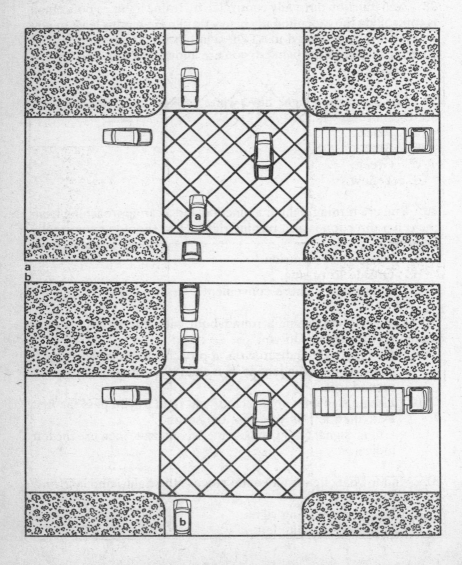

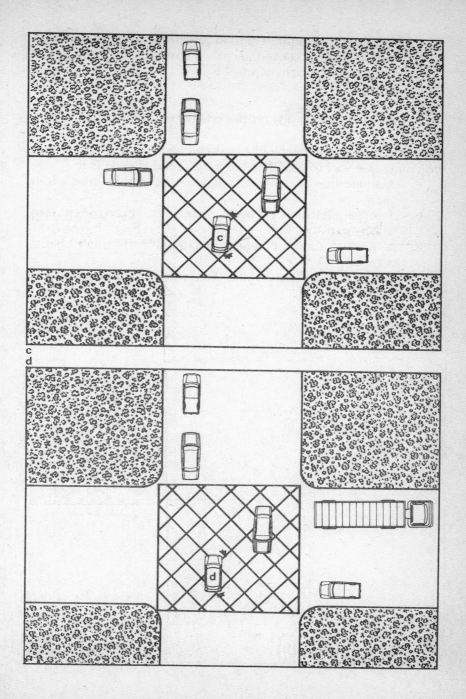

c

d

**34**  You are turning right at a road junction and you find that a pedestrian has already started to cross the road into which you are turning. Who has the right of way? Is it

    a.   You.

    b.   The pedestrian.

    c.   Neither; it depends on the conditions at the time.

**35**  Which of the following lines painted on the road indicate that you must give way to traffic on the major road ahead? Is it

    a.   A single line of white rectangles, spaced their own width apart.

    b.   Two parallel lines of white rectangles, spaced their own width apart.

    c.   A line of small, box-like rectangles with small spaces between.

    d.   A double line of small, box-like rectangles with small spaces between.

*Answers on page 201.*

# Parking and Waiting

**1** What is the sign for an official car park?

**2** Where are you allowed to park on a fast main road?

**3** What is a meter zone?

**4** Describe the sign that signifies a meter zone.

**5** You arrive at a meter zone outside meter hours. How must you park?

**6** What does the Code say about parking on the road at night?

**7** Cars and motorcycles may park on streets with a speed limit of 30 mph or less without lights at night. Which other two types of vehicles are included in this concession?

**8** Certain restrictions apply to this night-time parking without lights. What are they?

**9** When you are parking at night on a road not subject to a 30 mph speed limit, what lights must be showing?

**10** When are you allowed to park on the carriageway of a Clearway?

**11** What colour are the road markings that refer to parking or waiting?

**12** When you park on the road, what is your correct position?

**13**  When is it particularly dangerous to park on the road at night?

**14**  What precautions must you take before opening the door of your car?

**15**  Goods vehicles with a maximum weight of 7.5 tonnes are not normally allowed to park on any verge or central reservation. Describe the exception to this rule outlined in the Code.

**16**  Explain the reason for forbidding motorists to park opposite a traffic island.

**17**  Name five places where you should not park or wait because you would cause danger to other vehicles or pedestrians.

**18**  What precautions should you take for the safety of your passengers and yourself as you get out of your car on a busy road?

**19**  Whenever you plan to leave your vehicle you should switch off the engine and the headlamps and lock the vehicle. What has been omitted from this list?

**20**  Disabled drivers are allowed certain parking concessions. How would you know, from looking at his car, that the driver was disabled?

**21**  Under what circumstances are you allowed to let your vehicle stand within the area marked by zigzag lines on the approach to a pedestrian crossing?

**22**  In a road where parking is not allowed at any time, what markings would you expect to find along the edge of the carriageway?

**23**  You are not allowed to park where emergency vehicles go in and out. These include hospital, ambulance and doctors' entrances, police and fire stations and fire hydrants. What is omitted from this list?

**24**  If you see a bus pulling into a bus stop a short distance ahead, what should you do?

**25** You are hoping to park in a particular street but there is a line of parked cars down the right-hand side. There are no lines on the road forbidding you to park on the left but if you do so, the road will no longer be wide enough for large vehicles to pass. Your best course is to park with two of your wheels on the pavement to leave enough space. TRUE or FALSE?

**26** Day or night, you must always keep you lights on when parking in an underpass. TRUE or FALSE?

**27** Normally you are not allowed to park on roads marked down the centre with double white lines. The exception is when one of the lines is broken. TRUE or FALSE?

**28** If you are forced to park your car on the road on a foggy day, you should always leave your lights on. TRUE or FALSE?

**29** You are never allowed to park on the right hand side of the street at night. TRUE or FALSE?

**30** You are allowed to park in a cycle lane outside normal working hours. TRUE or FALSE?

**31** A sign tells you that you are on an Urban Clearway and lists the times that the Clearway operates on a nearby plate. During these times you are allowed to stop only long enough to set down or pick up passengers. TRUE or FALSE?

**32** Give the reasons why you should not park in the following places:
    a.   On a bend.
    b.   Near roadworks.
    c.   Near a bus stop.
    d.   In a passing place on a single track road.

**33** You are not allowed to park your vehicle on common land less than a certain distance from the highway. Is this distance
    a.   10 metres (33 ft).
    b.   15 metres (49 ft).
    c.   20 metres (66 ft).

**34** You may park your car opposite another car, even though this narrows the road. This is legal so long as it does not narrow the road more than a certain amount. Is this

    a.   The width of two vehicles.

    b.   The width of three vehicles.

    c.   The width of four vehicles.

**35** A plate at the roadside tells you: 'No loading Mon–Sat 8.30–6.30 pm.' How many yellow lines would you expect to find painted over the kerb?

    a.   One.

    b.   Two.

    c.   Three.

**36** What is the colour of the plate indicating that waiting is limited to a certain amount of time? Is it

    a.   Yellow.

    b.   Blue.

    c.   White.

*Answers on page 204.*

# The Law and You

**1**  What Act of Parliament controls vehicle licensing?

**2**  Name four documents you need before you can take your car on the road.

**3**  What must you ensure about your licence before you drive a vehicle?

**4**  When you receive your licence, what should you do before putting it away?

**5**  By law, who must wear seat belts?

**6**  You plan to borrow someone else's vehicle for a day trip to the country. When you are making arrangements with the owner, what should you check?

**7**  On a road where the normal speed limit is 70 mph, under what circumstances are you not entitled to drive at 70 mph?

**8**  What are the legal requirements about windscreens and windscreen wipers?

**9**  In what circumstances would you pick up a hitchhiker on the motorway?

**10**  Under certain conditions you are not allowed to sound your horn. What are they?

**11** The Highway Code gives four examples of the way in which alcohol may affect your driving ability. Name them.

**12** You have just begun a course of treatment prescribed by your doctor and you are not yet certain about the side effects of the medication you are taking. Before driving, what should you do?

**13** A dog dashes in front of you and you cannot avoid it. Unfortunately, the dog is killed in the collision. What must you do?

**14** You can be required to stop by a uniformed policeman or a traffic warden. Who else can require you to stop?

**15** What must a cyclist do before cycling on the road?

**16** If you are driving a vehicle carrying a load, what must you ensure?

**17** What is the rule on exhaust systems?

**18** What is the legal breath alcohol limit for drivers?

**19** What penalties can you expect for driving when over the legal limit for alcohol?

**20** Your car is difficult to start because of the cold. At last you set off, but you want to stop at the shop on the corner for a newspaper. You are afraid that if you stop the engine, it may not start again, so you leave the engine running for a couple of minutes while you collect your paper. Are you committing an offence?

**21** The code names four areas where you are not allowed to park on the motorway. Name them.

**22** What is the regulation about mirrors?

**23** What depth of tread must your tyres have as a legal minimum?

**24** Apart from wearing one, what must a driver do in relation to seat belts?

**25** What are the regulations for carrying a passenger on a motorcycle?

**26** Where must motorcyclists park in a meter zone?

**27** You are overtaking several slow vehicles travelling nose to tail along a country road. There is a broken white line down the centre of the road, so you pull out to overtake. As you are in the process of overtaking the vehicle at the head of the column, the road markings change, so that you are straddling a solid white line. Have you committed an offence?

**28** Your car has broken down on the motorway and you have to walk to the nearest phone. Where are you *forbidden* to walk?

**29** The maximum motorway speed for vans exceeding 2 tonnes maximum laden weight is 60 mph. TRUE or FALSE?

**30** On dual carriageways, coaches and goods vehicles not exceeding 7.5 tonnes are subject to the same speed limit. TRUE or FALSE?

**31** For your driving test, you must be able to read a car number plate at the prescribed distance without glasses. TRUE or FALSE?

**32** About one third of all pedestrians killed in road accidents have alcohol levels above the legal limit for driving. TRUE or FALSE?

**33** About 40 percent of all drivers killed in road accidents have alcohol levels above the legal limit of alcohol. TRUE or FALSE?

**34** You have bought a new tax disc but have not got around to displaying it on your car. You are committing an offence and can be fined. TRUE or FALSE?

**35** When you are instructing a learner driver who is reversing, you do not have to wear your seat belt. TRUE or FALSE?

**36** A pedal cyclist who has dismounted and is wheeling his or her cycle must still obey the traffic lights. TRUE or FALSE?

**37**  The legal blood alcohol limit for drivers is 85 mg of alcohol to 100 ml of blood. TRUE or FALSE?

**38**  Your car is parked in the road but it has broken down and you cannot afford the repairs. While you are still saving up to meet the bill, the tax disc runs out. Does this mean
    a.   That you are committing no offence as long as you do not drive the car.
    b.   That you are committing no offence as long as the car *cannot* be driven.
    c.   That you are committing an offence.

**39**  You are giving a relative driving lessons in your car at weekends. During the week you use the car for work. When you are using the car without a learner driver at the wheel, should you
    a.   Cover the L plates.
    b.   Remove the L plates.
    c.   Leave them as they are ready for the next lesson.

**40**  The police stop you because one of your rear lights is not working and ask for your driving licence and insurance certificate. You have your licence with you, but have left your insurance certificate at home. How long do you have to produce them at a police station? Is it
    a.   Three days.
    b.   Five days.
    c.   Seven days.

**41**  You should not stop your vehicle on the approach side of a pelican crossing beyond the double line of studs in the road, but there are certain exceptions to this rule. Are they
    a.   When you are stopping to obey signals.
    b.   You are loading or unloading.
    c.   When you need to do so to avoid an accident.
    d.   When you are waiting to turn right or left.

**42**  Are you committing an offence if the following are not in working order
    a.   Horn.
    b.   Speedometer.

   c.   Fog lamps.

   d.   Braking lights.

**43**  The Highway Code says that the wearing of seat belts can reduce the risk of death or injury in an accident. Is this reduction

   a.   One third.

   b.   Half.

   c.   Three-quarters.

**44**  Which of the following are exempt from wearing seat belts when travelling in the front seat of a car

   a.   Those holding exemption certificates.

   b.   Drivers who are reversing.

   c.   Adults under five feet tall.

   d.   Children under 14.

   e.   Local delivery drivers in vehicles built for the purpose.

**45**  You have a car phone in your vehicle and a call comes through while you are travelling along the motorway. Should you

   a.   Stop on the hard shoulder before taking the call.

   b.   Move into the nearside lane and drive slowly while taking the call.

   c.   Ignore the call.

**46**  You are driving a vehicle towing a trailer on a three- lane motorway. The nearside lane is blocked by slow moving lorries and the centre lane traffic is moving more slowly than you want to travel. Do you

   a.   Overtake.

   b.   Stay in the middle lane.

*Answers on page 207.*

# Other Road Users

1   What is a pelican crossing?

2   How does a zebra crossing differ from a pelican crossing?

3   Name two things that are not allowed in the area of the zigzag markings before a pedestrian crossing.

4   What must you avoid doing while waiting for pedestrians to cross?

5   How might you treat a zebra crossing with an island in the middle?

6   You are approaching a pedestrian crossing controlled by lights when the amber light shows. Under what circumstances can you drive on?

7   When there is no footpath, where should pedestrians walk?

8   Name three triangular warning signs with black silhouettes of people.

9   What is the rule on safety helmets for motor-cycle riders and passengers?

10   When is it specially important for pedestrians to wear clothes that can be seen easily when walking in the dark?

11   At a zebra crossing, how do you let pedestrians know that you are about to stop for them?

**12** When driving you might meet a marching troop or procession on the road. What precautions should you take?

**13** Name four groups of pedestrians who need extra care and consideration on the part of motorists.

**14** What rear markings are carried by heavy goods vehicles?

**15** At what times is your car allowed to use the bus lane?

**16** You are approaching traffic lights when the top light shows red and the middle light shows amber. What should you do?

**17** Describe the sign that indicates a parking place for caravans.

**18** If you are driving a slow-moving vehicle along a narrow winding road, in what way should you show consideration to the drivers who are following you?

**19** Blind pedestrians sometimes carry white sticks so that you can identify them. What type of stick would a deaf– blind person carry?

**20** If you were about to ride across a level crossing on horseback and you heard the warning begin to sound, what action would you take in the following circumstances
    a.   If you were approaching the crossing at the time.
    b.   If you were already on the crossing.

**21** As a cyclist, when are you allowed to remove one of your hands from the handlebars?

**22** Under what circumstances is a cyclist allowed to carry a passenger?

**23** When driving in the country, you may meet herds of animals. Where should you be specially careful in case you meet such a herd?

**24** What are pedestrians forbidden to do on pedestrian crossings?

**25** What pictorial symbol is used in the diamond- shaped sign on a vehicle carrying a spontaneously combustible substance?

**26** A special projection marker must be carried at the end of a load that overhangs the rear of the vehicle by a certain length. What is that length?

**27** Describe the marker mentioned in question 26.

**28** What lights should a group of marchers on the road carry at night?

**29** If the column of walkers is very long, what additional precautions should be taken?

**30** Apart from pedestrian crossings, where should drivers take special care in case pedestrians are crossing the road?

**31** Apart from helmets, what should motor-cyclists wear?

**32** Where should pedestrians never walk?

**33** Cyclists must *never* ride on the footpath or pavement. TRUE or FALSE?

**34** A cyclist should never lead a dog alongside the bike. TRUE or FALSE?

**35** When a cycle lane is marked by a sign and a broken white line it is an offence to drive or park a vehicle in that lane. TRUE or FALSE?

**36** Motor vehicles over 7500 kilograms (7½ tons) maximum gross weight are classified as heavy goods vehicles. TRUE or FALSE?

**37** Trailers over 3000 kilograms (3 tons) maximum gross weight are also classified as heavy goods vehicles. TRUE or FALSE?

**38** As a car driver, you should give way to a bus which is indicating its intention of moving out from a bus stop. TRUE or FALSE?

**39** Pedestrians and motor-cyclists should wear fluorescent material in the dark so that they can be seen more easily. TRUE or FALSE?

**40** Horse riders are only allowed to take their horses on the footpath if they dismount and lead their horses. TRUE or FALSE?

**41** At pedestrian crossings patrolled by lights drivers must give way to pedestrians who are still crossing when the signal allows vehicles to move. TRUE or FALSE?

**42** Under what circumstances must drivers stop for pedestrians at zebra crossings? Is it
  a.  Once they have stepped out onto the crossing.
  b.  When they are waiting at the kerb.

**43** At a pelican crossing, what does a flashing signal showing a green man mean? Does it mean that
  a.  Pedestrians can cross safely.
  b.  Pedestrians should not start to cross but those who have started can continue to cross the road.
  c.  Pedestrians who have already stepped into the road but have not reached the centre should turn back and wait on the pavement.

**44** Which of these vehicles are prohibited on the motorway?
  a.  Cars driven by learner drivers.
  b.  Tractors.
  c.  Motorcycles.
  d.  Cars towing caravans.
  e.  Invalid carriages.

**45** In which of these situations are you allowed to sound your horn:
  a.  When another driver overtakes and cuts in front of you, causing you to brake hard.
  b.  When you are calling for someone who is taking far too long getting ready.
  c.  When you want to warn a driver who is about to pull out into the road, unaware that you are approaching.
  d.  When the traffic lights have changed to green but the driver in front of you has not noticed.

*Answers on page 211.*

# Rules of the Road

**1**   As a careful driver, what speed limit should you always observe?

**2**   How would a cyclist make a right turn on a busy road at night?

**3**   You reach a level crossing with gates but no attendant. It has a STOP sign and small red and green lights. The green light is showing. How would you negotiate the crossing?

**4**   Your car has broken down on the highway. What ways are open to you to warn other traffic of the obstruction?

**5**   What is the two second rule?

**6**   Is there a time when you would be committing an offence by opening your car door?

**7**   You must not overtake where you might come into conflict with other road users: at road junctions, on the approach to pedestrian crossings, at level crossings and two other places. Can you name them?

**8**   What is the rule about your position when driving?

**9**   When a policemen is controlling the traffic ahead, what do you do?

**10**   When should you give way to pedestrians?

**11**   You are driving a large car and want to turn right from a side road onto a busy dual carriageway but the central reserve is too narrow to allow your car to pause safely. What do you do?

**12** Describe the marking that indicates the edges of driving lanes.

**13** Name three colours or combinations of traffic lights that mean STOP.

**14** What is an 'open' level crossing?

**15** You are driving in a strange town at night and, though you see no speed restriction notices, you know that you are in a 30 mph zone. How do you know?

**16** You pass several riders on horseback, leading riderless horses. Which horses should be closer to you, those with riders or those being led?

**17** What does the Code say about carrying things on a bicycle?

**18** You are driving on an unfamiliar road soon after a snowstorm. As you approach a major road, you find that the road sign is covered with snow so that you cannot read it. How do you know whether it is a Stop sign or a 'Give Way' sign?

**19** If you are in charge of a goods vehicle of over 3 tonnes unladen weight, where are you forbidden to park?

**20** You are approaching a zebra crossing with an island in the middle. There are no pedestrians on the left hand side of the crossing but two people are half way across the right hand side of the crossing, so you must stop. TRUE or FALSE?

**21** It is an offence to drive your vehicle in reverse more than necessary. TRUE or FALSE?

**22** When a policeman is controlling traffic at a junction with a STOP line, you must always stop at the line. TRUE or FALSE?

**23** On dual carriageways, buses and coaches are subject to a 60 mph speed limit. TRUE or FALSE?

**24** Learner drivers are not allowed to drive at more than 60 mph. TRUE or FALSE?

**25** At a level crossing with barriers, you need stop only when the red STOP lights begin to flash. TRUE or FALSE?

**26** When you pass a 'Road Works' sign and find that the repairs are all on your side of the road, you should give way to oncoming traffic. TRUE or FALSE?

**27** What do the following road signs mean?
   a.  A circular sign with a red border containing a number and the letter T.
   b.  A circular sign with a red border containing the numbers 7'-6".
   c.  A circular sign with a red border containing a silhouette of a lorry with numbers, e.g. 7.5T, on its side.
   d.  A circular sign with a red border containing a silhouette of a lorry and figures, e.g. 32 feet, beneath it, with arrows on each side.

**28** If you are riding a horse what should you wear
   a.  At all times.
   b.  In the dark.

**29** You see an area of diagonal white stripes on the road. Do they mean
   a.  That special care must be taken when overtaking.
   b.  That you should not drive over them if you can avoid it.
   c.  That traffic turning right must be extra careful.

**30** On a level crossing a blue sign says that drivers of large or slow vehicles must phone and get permission to cross. What does slow mean in this context? Is it
   a.  5 mph or less.
   b.  10 mph or less.
   c.  15 mph or less.

**31** In the sign described above, what does 'large' mean in terms of weight? Is it

a.   30 tonnes total weight.
b.   38 tonnes total weight.
c.   40 tonnes total weight.
d.   44 tonnes total weight.

**32**   You are driving at 50 mph on the open road on a fine day when another car overtakes you and pulls in about 55 metres (180 ft) ahead of you. Do you
a.   Maintain your speed.
b.   Increase your speed.
c.   Decrease speed.

**33**   What do the following road signs tell you?

**34**   You have stopped behind another vehicle at a STOP sign. As the driver in front pulls into the main road, do you
a.   Follow him across.
b.   Move up to the line and stop.
c.   Pause at the line but carry on if the road is clear.

**35** In one way streets where should a rider on horseback ride? Is it
  a.   On the right, against the traffic.
  b.   On the left, in the direction of the traffic.
  c.   On the pavement.

**36** Countdown markers indicate the distance from a concealed level crossing. What colour are they? Is it
  a.   Red with yellow bars.
  b.   Yellow with red bars.
  c.   White with red bars.
  d.   Red with white bars.

**37** What is the maximum speed limit for vans exceeding two tonnes maximum laden weight on single carriageways. Is it
  a.   40 mph.
  b.   50 mph.
  c.   60 mph.

*Answers on page 215.*

# Motorway Driving

**1** Which vehicles are prohibited on motorways?

**2** What sign is used to indicate the start of a motorway?

**3** Before setting off on a motorway journey, what checks should you make on your vehicle?

**4** Motorway speeds are higher than those on ordinary roads. In view of this, what will you need to do?

**5** Name four manoeuvres which you are forbidden to take on the motorway?

**6** What are slip roads?

**7** What is an acceleration lane and how do you use it?

**8** What is the speed limit on motorways?

**9** How do you prevent yourself feeling sleepy while driving on motorways?

**10** Once you have joined the motorway, how long should you stay in the left-hand lane?

**11** Some vehicles are forbidden to use the right-hand lane of a motorway with three or more lanes. Can you name them?

**12** When are motorway drivers allowed to stop on the hard shoulder?

**13** You are travelling along a three-lane motorway and you pull out into the middle lane to overtake slower traffic. Under what circumstances are you allowed to continue to travel in the middle lane?

**14** You see a sign reading: A46 (M69). What does this sign tell you?

**15** What is the right-hand lane of a three lane carriageway used for?

**16** What do green studs mark on the motorway?

**17** Name four situations when you can stop your car on the motorway.

**18** Under what conditions are you allowed to overtake on the left on a motorway?

**19** Where is parking permitted on motorways?

**20** What hazards do link roads and slip roads present and how do you cope with them?

**21** Give details of the correct procedure for overtaking on a motorway?

**22** Under what conditions should you be extra careful about overtaking?

**23** Where would you find a deceleration lane on a motorway and what is its purpose?

**24** What is the first thing to do when your car breaks down on a motorway?

**25** How can you tell where to find the nearest telephone?

**26** One type of accident occurs more frequently on motorways than any other. What is this kind of accident?

**27** What do you do if you see a red light flashing above the lane in which you are travelling or on the entrance to a slip road?

**28** Why should you be extra careful to watch your speedometer as you leave the motorway?

**29** What is the sign that indicates that the motorway is coming to an end?

**30** When you are joining the motorway from the slip road and acceleration lane and the traffic is too heavy to allow a suitable gap, drivers approaching in the left-hand lane are obliged to give way for you. TRUE or FALSE?

**31** Red-coloured studs mark the left-hand edge of the carriageway. TRUE or FALSE?

**32** Learner drivers can use motorways only when accompanied by a qualified driving instructor. TRUE or FALSE?

**33** You are not allowed to use the hard shoulder for overtaking. TRUE or FALSE?

**34** It is an offence to set down a passenger on any part of the motorway, except for the slip-road. TRUE or FALSE?

**35** When your car is stationary after a breakdown, you should make sure that your passengers always remain inside the vehicle. TRUE or FALSE?

**36** A suitcase falls from the roof of your car and you are afraid that it will cause danger to other motorists. Should you
a. Do your best to retrieve it immediately.
b. Leave it where it is while you notify the police on the roadside telephone.

**37** You are driving in the centre lane of a three lane carriageway and the drive rin front is keeping just below the speed limit and slowing you down. You know that passing him will take you over the speed limit. Do you

a. Pull into the outside lane, exceeding the speed limit for only as long as it takes to get past.
b. Stay where you are.
c. Keep blowing your horn until the driver in front realises that he is creating a nuisance.

**38** You pass a motorway exit only to realise immediately afterwards that you should have taken it. You know that the next exit is 15 miles away. Do you
a. Carry on to the next exit.
b. Reverse only if the left-hand lane behind you is completely clear.
c. Reverse along the hard shoulder.

**39** You are driving on a two-lane carriageway and you pull out into the right-hand lane to overtake a lorry. You can see that there are a number of slow-moving vehicles ahead in the left-hand lane. Do you
a. Return to the left-hand lane until it is necessary to overtake the next vehicle.
b. Stay in the right-hand lane.

**40** You see a red triangle on the hard shoulder. Does this mean
a. A broken down vehicle 100 metres (328 ft) ahead.
b. A broken down vehicle 150 metres (492 ft) ahead.
c. Road works ahead.
d. Further warning signs ahead.

**41** When rejoining the carriageway after an emergency stop, you should
a. Use the hard shoulder to build up speed while you wait for a suitable gap in the traffic.
b. Wait until there is sufficient space to pull out into the left-hand lane and build up speed there.

**42** You enter a motorway to find amber lights flashing at regular intervals. Should you
a. Drive at normal speed but keep on the alert for further signals.

b.  Drive at under 50 mph until you are certain that it is safe to increase speed.
c.  Drive at under 30 mph until you are certain that it is safe to increase speed.

**43**  Road signals on motorways are placed:
a.  On the central reservation.
b.  On the left hand side.
c.  Overhead.

*Answers on page 218*

# Lights and Signals

**1**  You are waiting at an automatic half barrier level crossing. A train passes but the barrier stays down and the lights continue to flash. What does this mean?

**2**  As a motorist, when would you use arm signals?

**3**  What light signals would show you that the driver in front was slowing down?

**4**  When are the light or arm signals to show that you are slowing down specially important?

**5**  At a pelican crossing controlled by traffic lights, what follows red?

**6**  When this light is showing, what should drivers do?

**7**  Name three categories of people with authority to control traffic.

**8**  What sign would you expect to find on the road if the traffic lights are out of action?

**9**  Name five places where you might see alternately flashing red lights?

**10**  You see flashing blue lights ahead. What action should you take?

**11**  You are planning a long drive at night, so you check your

164

head and side lights, your tail lights and indicators, as well as your fog lamps. Which lights have you omitted to check?

**12** Once you have checked that all your lamps work, what other aspect of your lighting should you check?

**13** Your journey takes you along unfamiliar roads without street lighting and you are using full headlights. When would you dip them?

**14** What is the difference between the Go sign on road traffic lights and the Go signal at an automatic 'open' level crossing?

**15** What is the difference between the operation of regular traffic lights and the lights at pelican crossings?

**16** Dusk is approaching and the tail lights of the car ahead of you come on. How do you know whether the driver has just switched on his side and rear lights or is braking, in which case you need to adjust your driving accordingly?

**17** Why are you not allowed to park or wait near traffic lights?

**18** In the traffic light sequence
 a. What follows red?
 b. What follows green?
 c. What follows red and amber?

**19** The car in front of you on the road has its left-hand amber winker going. This may mean that the driver plans to turn left. What else could it mean?

**20** What arm signals would you give to a policeman controlling traffic if you wanted to
 a. Turn left.
 b. Turn right.

**21** What lights would you expect those herding cattle on the road after sunset to use?

**22** You are waiting at a junction to cross a major road. Only one car is approaching from the right and the driver is flashing his left hand indicator. What precautions do you take?

**23**  It is a dark, rainy night, so visibility is fairly poor. Under these conditions, it is a good idea to use your rear fog lamps. TRUE or FALSE?

**24**  You are already on a level crossing when the amber lights flash and the alarm sounds. Providing that the road behind you is clear, the safest thing to do is to stop and reverse. TRUE or FALSE?

**25**  Horse riders should give the same arm signals as motorcyclists. TRUE or FALSE?

**26**  You should always move off promptly when the traffic lights show green. TRUE or FALSE?

**27**  When the traffic lights change from red to red and amber you should move off slowly. TRUE or FALSE?

**28**  When you draw into the side of the road to make a delivery, you should switch on your hazard warning lights. TRUE or FALSE?

**29**  When you are approaching a junction controlled by a policeman you must give the appropriate signal if you want to turn right or left. If you are going straight ahead, you do not need to give a signal. TRUE or FALSE?

**30**  In an area where you are allowed to park your vehicle without lights at night, it must not be parked within 20 metres (65 ft) of a road junction. TRUE or FALSE?

**31**  In the traffic light sequence, amber is followed by red. TRUE or FALSE?

**32**  You have stopped at the red light at a crossroads. After a few minutes, it becomes obvious that the lights have stuck. When this happens, you can legally drive on against the red light. TRUE or FALSE?

**33**   When a motorcyclist intends to turn left he will extend his right arm and make a circling movement. TRUE or FALSE?

**34**   When you are travelling on a motorway with good overhead lighting you should use
   a.   Side lights.
   b.   Dipped headlights.
   c.   Full beam.

**35**   You are approaching traffic lights when the amber light shows. Should you
   a.   Accelerate to make sure of being safely across before they turn red.
   b.   Slow and be ready to stop if the lights turn red.
   c.   Stop.

**36**   You are driving along a road with cars parked on both sides, leaving only one car's width down the middle. A driver approaching from the opposite direction flashes his headlamps at you. Do you assume
   a.   That he means to drive on.
   b.   That he is giving you priority and you should drive on.
   c.   Neither.

**37**   You must use headlamps or fog lamps when visibility is seriously reduced. According to the Code, does 'seriously reduced' mean
   a.   Less than 75 metres (246 ft).
   b.   Less than 100 metres (328 ft).
   c.   Less than 150 metres (492 ft).

**38**   The traffic lights are red but a green arrow at the side points left. Does this mean
   a.   Traffic turning left can filter, regardless of the main traffic lights.
   b.   Traffic turning left can filter only when the green light shows on the main traffic lights.
   c.   Traffic turning right must stop but traffic going straight on and traffic turning left may proceed.

**39**  You are forbidden to sound your horn in a built-up area between certain times. Is it

    a.    22.00 and 07.00 (10 p.m. and 7 a.m.).

    b.    23.00 and 06.00 (11 p.m. and 6 a.m.).

    c.    23.30 and 07.00 (11.30 p.m. and 7 a.m.).

    d.    Lighting up time and sunrise.

**40**  When driving at night, you must use your headlamps on roads without street lighting. You must also use them on roads where the street lamps are more than a certain distance apart. Is this distance

    a.    150 metres (492 ft).

    b.    175 metres (574 ft).

    c.    185 metres (607 ft).

    d.    200 metres (656 ft).

**41**  What two things are indicated by motorists making each of the following arm signals?

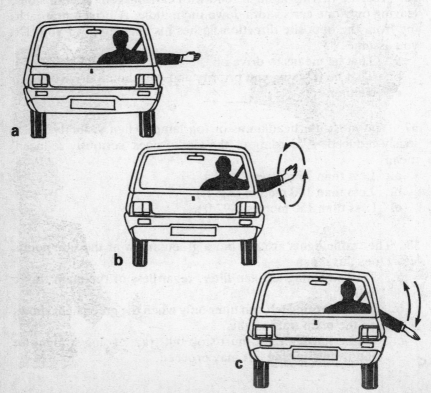

**42** What do the following signals mean from a policeman controlling traffic?

*Answers on page 222.*

a

b

c

d

e

# Safety on the Road

**1** According to the Code, there is only one meaning for flashing headlights. What is it?

**2** Where would you find hazard warning posts?

**3** What colour are the reflectors on the nearside hazard posts?

**4** What colour are the offside reflectors?

**5** Name four types of road on which you must use your headlamps at night.

**6** What is the 'thinking distance'?

**7** What is the 'braking distance'?

**8** On a foggy day, what should you switch on apart from your lights?

**9** What is the safest place for a young child to travel in the car?

**10** Your car is involved in an accident and you have to wait for the emergency services. You have no passengers in the car but the family dog is travelling with you. What should you do with the dog while you wait?

**11** How would you expect a responsible cyclist wheeling a cycle at night to behave?

**12** The Code says that motorists should pay particular attention to

lights, brakes, steering, seat belts, windscreen wipers and washers –
and two other things. What are they?

**13** What *must* you do whenever you leave your vehicle?

**14** According to the Code, what special care must you take when
passing roadworks on the motorway?

**15** You should never drive when under the influence of alcohol or
drugs. What two other physical conditions should make you post-
pone a planned drive?

**16** Apart from providing suitable restraints, what extra precautions can you take for the safety of the children travelling in
your car?

**17** What three things should you do as you drive past a school?

**18** What extra precautions should a motorist take when driving in
wet weather?

**19** How should a driver approach a pedestrian crossing?

**20** Name four places where you are not allowed to park because it
would obscure the view of other drivers.

**21** What should every cyclist using the road remember?

**22** On fast roads, you need to take special care before pulling out
to overtake. Why?

**23** Where would you be likely to see yellow zigzags at the edge of
the road and what do they mean?

**24** You have been driving on the motorway for some time and you
begin to feel sleepy. What do you do?

**25** Why is it dangerous to follow the tail-lights of the vehicle in
front in fog?

**26** Under what conditions would you use main beam headlights?

**27** What parts of the vehicle should you always keep clean to ensure safety?

**28** Why should you be particularly careful when approaching a low bridge across the road?

**29** After a motorway accident, you are helping to get dazed but injured passengers out of the vehicles involved. For their safety, what must you ensure?

**30** If an accident involves a vehicle containing dangerous goods and displaying a hazard warning sign, what are the special dangers you must keep in mind?

**31** At a level crossing with gates but no red lights and no attendant, you telephone the signalman to make sure that it is safe to cross, then open both gates. What must you do after that?

**32** What are the regulations on tyres outlined in the Code?

**33** What picture would you expect to see on the diamond shaped hazard sign displayed by a lorry carrying a corrosive substance?

**34** You are approaching a pedestrian crossing with one vehicle ahead of you. A pedestrian is waiting on the kerb and the car in front of you slows, presumably preparing to stop. It would be an offence if you overtook the vehicle in front. TRUE or FALSE?

**35** You are allowed to carry children in the luggage space behind the back seat of an estate car providing they sit with their backs to the engine. TRUE or FALSE?

**36** It is legal for a two year old child to wear an adult seat belt. TRUE or FALSE?

**37** You must never sound your horn when your vehicle is stationary. TRUE or FALSE?

**38** You need glasses to read number plates at the prescribed distance. To stay within the law, you must wear them when you drive. TRUE or FALSE?

**39** You are carrying a nine year old child in the back of the car where you have adult seat belts fitted but no child safety harness. You can make sure that the child is safe by boosting her height with an ordinary household cushion. TRUE or FALSE?

**40** If you are driving at 20 mph, your overall stopping distance is 12m (40 ft). In this case your thinking and braking distance would be about the same. TRUE or FALSE?

**41** Your car is in a queue of traffic approaching a pedestrian crossing at a snail's pace. You must not drive onto the crossing until your exit is clear. TRUE or FALSE?

**42** What is the maximum speed for cars in the following areas
  a. Built-up areas.
  b. Single carriageway roads outside built-up areas.
  c. Dual carriageways.

**43** You are going on holiday, towing your caravan behind your car. When you are travelling on a single carriageway road in open country, what is your maximum speed limit? Is it
  a. 40 mph.
  b. 50 mph.
  c. 60 mph.
  d. 70 mph.

**44** You are carrying a seven year old child in your car but you have no restraints fitted in the rear. Is it safer for the child to travel
  a. In the rear.
  b. In the front with an adult seat belt.
  c. In the front with an adult seat belt and booster cushion.

**45** The Code specifies the safest method of child restraint for infants under nine months. Is it
  a. A carry cot secured with special straps.
  b. A rear facing infant safety seat.
  c. A child safety harness.
  d. A child safety seat.

**46** If you are travelling at 60 mph (assuming that the road is dry, that brakes and tyres are in good order) how much greater is your overall stopping distance than a similar car travelling at 40 mph? Is it

a.   Half as far again.
b.   Twice as far.
c.   Nearly three times as far.

**47**   The Code recommends using a child safety seat for children up to a certain age group. Is this age group

a.   Three or four.
b.   Four or five.
c.   Five or six.

**48**   What picture would you expect to see on the hazard warning sign displayed by a lorry carrying radioactive material. Is it

a.   A circle attached to a flat base, with black flames rising from the top.
b.   Three black triangles with their points trimmed off, arranged round a black dot.
c.   A skull and crossbones, resting on the top of a mushroom-shaped cloud.

*Answers on page 226.*

# Driving Techniques

**1** When is it most difficult to judge the speed of approaching vehicles?

**2** What is the first rule governing overtaking?

**3** Once you have started to overtake, what should you do?

**4** When you are overtaking a motorcyclist, how much clearance should you give?

**5** How often should you look in the mirror while driving?

**6** Name four instances where it is *essential* to check your mirror.

**7** You are riding a motorcycle and want to overtake the vehicle in front. Before signalling that you want to move out, what should you do?

**8** You are cruising at a steady speed when a child runs out into the road in pursuit of a ball. You make an emergency stop and come to a halt in 23 metres (75 ft). What was your speed?

**9** What poor driving techniques might cause skidding?

**10** You plan to leave the motorway at the next exit. Describe the sequence of actions you should take.

**11** Name three situations when you must *not* reverse.

**12** What must you do before you reverse?

**13** What is the 'blind area'?

**14** If you are planning to reverse and find that you cannot see clearly, what should you do?

**15** What sequence should you always remember when planning to overtake, turn or stop?

**16** The 'One Way' sign and the 'Ahead Only' sign both have blue backgrounds and white arrows pointing ahead. What is the difference between the signs?

**17** Motorists need to remember that cyclists may not be able to keep a straight course. Under what conditions might you find them wavering?

**18** What should motorcyclists look out for when overtaking queues of traffic?

**19** What three things must you never do on a level crossing?

**20** You are turning right and after giving your signal you are moving to take up your position near the centre of the road. As you make your manoeuvre, what consideration should you give to other vehicles?

**21** When driving on country roads without footpaths, where should you take special care in case you meet pedestrians walking in the road?

**22** The Code says that you should move off only 'when you can do so safely without . . . ' Complete this sentence.

**23** You are turning left into a side road from a main highway, following the approved procedure. When you have completed your manoeuvre, what must you remember to do?

**24** You should never overtake a cyclist or motorcyclist immediately before turning left. TRUE or FALSE?

**25** You should never overtake when doing so would force another vehicle to slow down. TRUE or FALSE?

**26**  You are only allowed to reverse from a side road into a main road if you have inadvertently entered a one-way street. TRUE or FALSE?

**27**  You are following a slow and irritating driver on the approach to a bend. Providing driving conditions are good and you can see that there is no oncoming traffic, it is permissible to overtake. TRUE or FALSE?

**28**  For 20 minutes you have been following a large and slow-moving lorry that obscures your view of the road ahead. At last the driver extends his arm from the window and waves you on. This means that it is safe to overtake. TRUE or FALSE?

**29**  Before moving off you should always use your mirror. When the road is busy, you should make a final check by looking round. TRUE or FALSE?

**30**  Study the diagram below. Two cars are parked on the left hand side of the road. Car A is approaching on the left, car B is approaching in the opposite direction. Which car has the right of way, car A or car B?

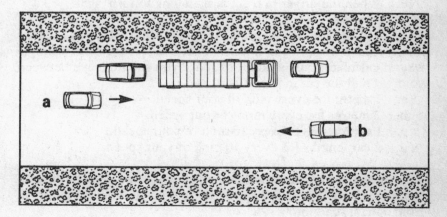

**31**  Why should you not overtake at or near the following
    a.   When approaching the brow of a hill.
    b.   Where the road narrows.
    c.   At a road junction.

**32**  If you have to move from one lane to another on the road, what must you do before starting your manoeuvre? Do you
a.  Accelerate.
b.  Glance in the mirror.
c.  Use your signal indicator.
d.  Sound your horn.

**33**  You are driving at the maximum speed you consider safe in the current road conditions when an impatient motorist behind starts flashing his lights and pulling out to overtake. Do you
a.  Increase your speed until he drops back.
b.  Continue at the same speed to discourage him.
c.  Decrease your speed and allow him to pass.

**34**  Normally you overtake on the right but there are exceptions. Are they
a.  In one way streets.
b.  When you are turning left at a junction.
c.  When the traffic is moving in slow queues and the queue on your right is moving more slowly than you.
d.  When vehicles in the right hand lane of a motorway refuse to move in and allow you to pass.
e.  When the driver in front is signalling to turn right.

**35**  The Code lists the shortest stopping distances for an average family saloon in good conditions. What does it suggest as a simple way of calculating the amount of space you should leave between your car and the car in front? Is it
a.  1 metre for every mph of your speed.
b.  2 metres for every mph of your speed.
c.  1 car length for every 10 mph of your speed.
d.  2 car lengths for every 10 mph of your speed.

**36**  Study the diagrams on the opposite page and decide which of the four drivers has taken up the correct position for a right turn from a main road into a side road.

*Answers on page 230.*

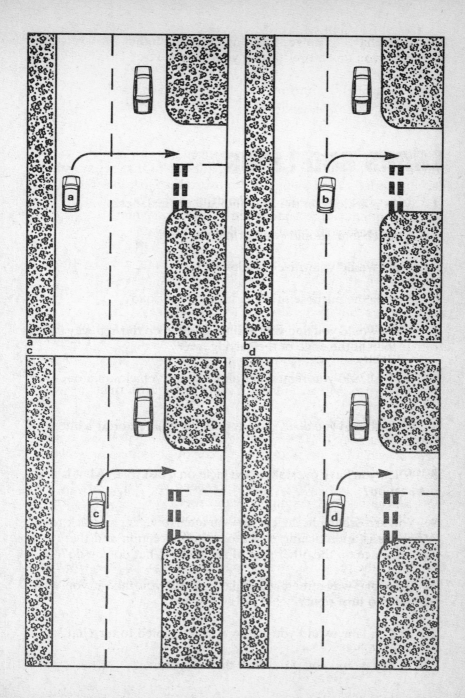

# Lanes and Lines

**1**  What markings on the road indicate traffic lanes?

**2**  In which lane should you normally travel?

**3**  When would you travel in another lane?

**4**  What is the purpose of white lines on the road?

**5**  When would you find yellow lines painted on the highway itself, rather than at the edge of the carriageway?

**6**  What should you remember about other vehicles in a one-way street?

**7**  What should you do as soon as possible after entering a one-way street?

**8**  When you have overtaken a vehicle on a fast road, what is your next action?

**9**  You are driving in the country on a narrow, single- track road. A vehicle is approaching in the opposite direction and there is a passing place on the other side of the road. What do you do?

**10**  In a one-way street, which lane would you take if you were planning to turn right?

**11**  Which lane would you follow if you planned to turn left?

**12**  When would you not follow the rules above?

**13** Direction signs positioned over motorways have arrows pointing downwards. What do they mean?

**14** When you are travelling in a one-way street, you might encounter a particular problem with bus lanes. What is it?

**15** Lane discipline is important for safe motoring; what should you always avoid?

**16** When coming to a junction, what would guide you in selecting a lane?

**17** All bus lanes operate for 24 hours. TRUE or FALSE?

**18** Cyclists can always use bus lanes. TRUE or FALSE?

**19** You are travelling on a single carriageway with four lanes. A stationary lorry is blocking the nearside lane and slow moving traffic on the outer lane on your side of the carriageway is slowing you down. If there are no vehicles coming in the opposite direction, you may use the outer lane on the right hand side of the carriageway to overtake. TRUE or FALSE?

**20** You must never drive in the middle of the road. TRUE or FALSE?

**21** It is an offence to drive in a cycle lane marked with a solid white line. TRUE or FALSE?

**22** You must never cross a hazard warning line. TRUE or FALSE?

**23** Coloured reflecting studs are often used with the white lines on the road. What is marked by the following colours
    a.  White.
    b.  Red.
    c.  Amber.
    d.  Green.

**24** The diagram below shows two cars preparing to turn off a fast highway. Which car is taking the correct route, car A or car B?

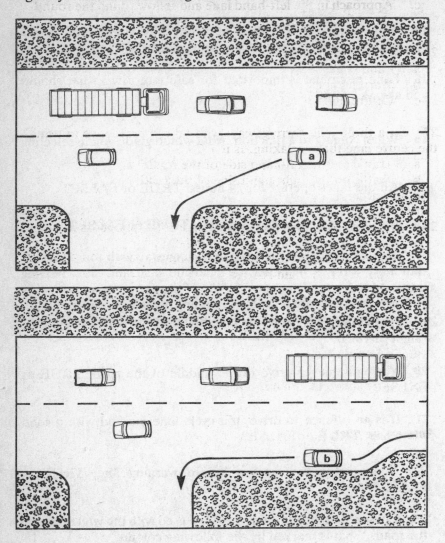

**25** You are approaching a roundabout and you intend to turn right. Do you

    a.   Approach in the right-hand lane, keep to that lane in the roundabout.

b.   Approach in the left-hand lane, switch to the right on the roundabout.

c.   Approach in the left-hand lane and follow round the roundabout in that lane.

**26**  How do you identify the following marking on the road:

a.   Lane lines.

b.   Warning lines.

c.   Centre lines.

**27**  On a three lane carriageway, who takes precedence in using the centre lane for overtaking. Is it

a.   Traffic on the left-hand side of the road.

b.   Traffic on the right-hand side of the road.

c.   Neither.

**28**  Which vehicles have precedence on a roundabout? Is it

a.   Vehicles approaching the roundabout.

b.   Vehicles already using the roundabout.

c.   Vehicles on a main A road.

d.   None of these.

**29**  In a one-way street, which lane do you take if you are going straight on? Is it

a.   The right lane.

b.   The left lane.

c.   Any convenient lane.

*Answers on page 233.*

# Breakdowns and Accidents

**1** Your car breaks down on the highway. What is your first priority?

**2** Your vehicle is safely parked after a breakdown. What is the chief danger you should keep in mind while waiting for assistance?

**3** Some cars are fitted with a special warning device. What is it?

**4** When there are no warning signs placed on the road, what other signs might suggest to you that an accident had taken place ahead?

**5** If you do see an accident ahead, what do you do?

**6** One of the chief dangers after a road accident is a further collision. What is the other?

**7** What steps should you take to prevent this?

**8** If you are first on the scene of an accident, what five actions should you take, in addition to the above?

**9** If you are first on the scene of a motorway accident, how do you summon help?

**10** If you are notifying the emergency services of an accident, what information do you need to give?

**11** If you are involved in an accident which results in injury to an animal you must stop. Which of the following animals is mentioned in the road traffic act?

| a. Dog. | c. Horse. | e. Sheep. |
|---------|-----------|-----------|
| b. Cat. | d. Pig.   | f. Goat.  |

**12** You come upon an accident involving a car and a lorry displaying a diamond-shaped sign. What does this sign mean?

**13** What additional action should you take when you are the first to reach such an accident?

**14** You are driving across an automatic half-barrier level crossing when your engine dies. You attempt to restart it without success and you are still trying when the alarm sounds and the lights flash to herald an approaching train. What do you do?

**15** Your car breaks down on a level crossing when there is no sign of a train approaching. What do you do?

**16** Describe how you can prepare yourself to give effective help in case of an accident where people may be injured?

**17** You are giving what help you can at the scene of an accident. One of the casualties is bleeding from a wound in the leg. What can you use to stop the bleeding?

**18** While you are trying to stop the bleeding what must you avoid doing?

**19** You arrive at the site of an accident, where a car has skidded off the road. The driver has crawled out of the car and is sitting at the roadside. You can see no obvious injury but he is obviously in a state of shock. What steps should you take to help?

**20** You are the driver of a car which is involved in an accident. No one is hurt but you have damaged a bollard in the middle of the road. What two things must you do?

**21** If you have not done both these things at the time, what must you do?

**22** It is an icy day in mid-winter and the casualties from a road accident are shivering with cold, even after they have been wrapped in overcoats. One helpful local resident offers them tea, another offers brandy. Which offer should be accepted?

**23**  You are driving through a town when you hear a siren behind you and see a vehicle with a blue lamp flashing. What do you do?

**24**  If traffic cones are used at the scene of a breakdown or accident, the first cone should be about 15 metres (49 ft) behind the vehicle involved. TRUE or FALSE?

**25**  The last cone should be 5 metres (16 ft) behind the vehicle. TRUE or FALSE?

**26**  You set off on holiday with your luggage and camping gear piled on the roof. As you are driving along a dual carriageway (not a motorway) your inflatable dinghy falls off into the road. Instead of trying to retrieve it, you should summon police assistance. TRUE or FALSE?

**27**  You are driving at 40 mph on the open road when you see a lorry blocking the carriageway ahead. The road is dry, your brakes are in good condition, so providing you have your wits about you, you should be able to make an emergency stop in 30 metres (98 ft). TRUE or FALSE?

**28**  At a serious accident, you prepare to give mouth to mouth resuscitation to a victim who has stopped breathing. Before you begin you should tilt the victim's head backwards. TRUE or FALSE?

**29**  You begin mouth to mouth resuscitation by pinching the victim's nostrils together, then blowing into the mouth until the chest rises. You then repeat this action every six seconds until the victim is breathing normally. TRUE or FALSE?

**30**  Your car has broken down on the motorway and you need to phone for assistance. You can see the nearest roadside phone on the other side of the motorway. Do you
 a.  Wait for a gap in the traffic then cross to use it.
 b.  Walk along the hard shoulder until you find the nearest phone on your side of the motorway.

**31** Your breakdown takes place at night. While you wait for assistance to arrive, where should you *not* stand?

    a.    At the side of your car on the road.
    b.    At the side of your car on the kerb.
    c.    At the front of your car.
    d.    At the back of your car.

**32** You are sensible enough to carry a red warning triangle in your car. When you use the triangle to warn other drivers that your car has broken down on an ordinary main road, where do you place the triangle?

    a.    Immediately behind your car.
    b.    30 metres (98 ft) behind your car.
    c.    50 metres (190 ft) behind your car.
    d.    100 metres (328 ft) behind your car.
    e.    150 metres (492 ft) behind your car.

**33** One of the casualties at the scene of an accident is bleeding from a leg wound but the leg is not broken. Should you

    a.    Raise his body so that it is higher than his leg.
    b.    Raise the leg so that it is higher than the body.
    c.    Leave well alone.

**34** You have been involved in an accident in which someone is injured but have not been able to produce your insurance certificate to the police at the time. How soon afterwards must you produce it:

    a.    Within three days.
    b.    Within five days.
    c.    Within seven days.

**35** You come upon an accident and find one of the drivers unconscious but breathing normally. Should you

    a.    Leave the injured driver where he is until medical help arrives.
    b.    Move him carefully so that you can make him more comfortable.

*Answers on page 235.*

# Miscellaneous

**1** Why is it specially important to keep checking your speeds on the motorway?

**2** At an automatic half barrier level crossing, the warning signals include an alarm. Where would you hear an alarm on signals on an ordinary road?

**3** Which other road users must you look out for particularly when both overtaking and turning – and why?

**4** You are turning right at a junction when an oncoming vehicle is also turning right and, because of the traffic situation at the time, you are not able to pass offside to offside. While you are passing nearside to nearside, what must you do?

**5** Are there any restrictions on the number of people who can be carried in an ordinary family saloon?

**6** Your exhaust is belching out black smoke as you drive along the highway. Are you committing an offence?

**7** If you are leaving children or pets in a parked car, what must you remember?

**8** For the sake of security, where should you park if you have to leave your car after dark?

**9** You park your car in a quiet side street for the day, while you catch the bus into town. To make sure your vehicle and its contents will be secure while you are gone, what four things must you do?

**10** You are moving off from a parked position at the kerbside. You check your mirrors, signal, then move off if it is safe to do so. What have you omitted to do?

**11** What three things should any sensible cyclist do when turning left or right?

**12** You are backing into a space in a car park when you inadvertently run into another car, damaging the wing. You are unable to locate the owner. What should you do?

**13** There are four different types of level crossings. Three of them are: automatic half barrier crossings, automatic open crossings and open level crossings. What is the fourth?

**14** What are the rules for overtaking on the motorway?

**15** What is the greatest danger that drivers leaving a motorway need to look out for?

**16** Before riding a horse on the highway, what should you ensure?

**17** When the road has recently been resurfaced, when the workmen have finished their job and moved on, what warning sign might you expect to see?

**18** You are travelling along a winding country road with a number of blind bends when a farm worker flags you down. What is the reason likely to be?

**19** You should always give way to emergency vehicles. How would you know that such a vehicle was approaching if it was still several vehicles behind in a line of traffic?

**20** What three important rules govern signalling?

**21** Where are invalid carriages not allowed?

**22** Where should you never carry children in cars?

**23** If one of your headlights is defective so that it is only giving off main beam, are you committing an offence?

**24** What is the speed rule you should always remember when driving in the dark?

**25** When should you use the special telephones provided at some level crossings?

**26** When you are negotiating a junction with two or even three roundabouts, what rule do you follow?

**27** In the situation described above, what must you look out for specially?

**28** You run into the back of another car, damaging the bumper. You exchange names and addresses and insurance details with the other driver. You must also inform the police. TRUE or FALSE?

**29** Your driving can be seriously affected if you have had a drink but are still well below the legal limit. TRUE or FALSE?

**30** A heavy goods vehicle (exceeding 7.5 tonnes) and a car towing a caravan both travelling along a dual carriageway, are subject to the same speed restriction. TRUE or FALSE?

**31** You are turning left at a roundabout so you signal left on approach and through the roundabout. TRUE or FALSE?

**32** It is an offence to dazzle other road users with your headlights. TRUE or FALSE?

**33** Your road fund licence has expired but your renewal application is in the post, so it is permissible to drive the car. TRUE or FALSE?

**34** Two out of three pedestrians killed or badly injured are under 15 or over 70. TRUE or FALSE?

**35** Cyclists should always ride single file on the highway. TRUE or FALSE?

**36** Some level crossings have no gates, barriers or lights but they do have a sign. Is it

a. Stop.
b. Give Way.
c. Reduce Speed.

**37** You are driving carefully, keeping a safe distance between your car and the vehicle in front, when a car overtakes you and slots into the gap. Do you
a. Maintain a steady speed.
b. Hoot or flash your lights to draw attention to his thoughtlessness.
c. Drop back.
d. Overtake the offending car.

**38** Special overhead signals on motorways have flashing amber lights. What does the sign in the middle of these lights indicate? Is it
a. Temporary maximum speed limits.
b. Do not proceed any further in this lane.
c. Change lane.
d. End of restriction.

**39** Your car is towing a trailer on a motorway journey. What is your maximum speed limit? Is it
a. 50 mph.
b. 60 mph.
c. 70 mph.

**40** What is the thinking distance for a motorist driving at the following speeds on dry roads?
a. 30 mph.
b. 50 mph.
c. 70 mph.

**41** What is the braking distance for a motorist driving at the following speeds on dry roads?
a. 30 mph.
b. 40 mph.
c. 60 mph.

*Answers on page 238.*

# Answers

## Signs and Markings

**1** Circular.

**2** Red.

**3** A thick white line separates the bus lane from the rest of the road and signs give details of times when the lane can be used by normal traffic.

**4** Zigzag lines on the road mark the area on the approach to zebra crossings where parking is forbidden.

**5** Lines along the edge of the carriageway indicate waiting restrictions. Lines painted on the kerb indicate loading and unloading restrictions.

**6**   a.  A level crossing with a barrier or gate.
      b.  A level crossing without a barrier or gate.

**7** Blue.

**8** Green.

**9**   a.  Crossroads ahead.
      b.  No overtaking allowed.
      c.  You can only drive straight ahead.
      d.  Pedestrian crossing ahead.
      e.  A quayside or river bank ahead.
      f.  No entry for vehicles.

g. Humps in the road.
h. Give way to traffic from the right at a mini roundabout.
i. Loose chippings in the road.
j. Maximum speed allowed 40 mph.
k. No motor vehicles except scooters, mopeds and solo motor cycles.
l. With-flow bicycle lane.

**10** They are warning signs.

**11** No stopping (clearway).

**12** A rectangular sign with a blue background and a large white letter H.

**13** You must drive carefully, avoid sounding your horn, give way to ambulances and take care never to obstruct entrances and exits.

**14**
a. The national speed limit applies.
b. There is no left turn.
c. All traffic should turn left.
d. Warning of a double bend ahead, first to the left.
e. Warning of a humped bridge ahead.
f. Warning of uneven road surface.
g. The number of available lanes ahead is permanently reduced.
h. Wild animals might cross the road.
i. The dual carriageway is about to end.
j. The traffic streams could be a danger to one another. Do not enter the hatched area if you can avoid it.
k. One way traffic ahead.
l. Do not enter the box junction marked on the road if your exit is not clear.

**15** Signs marking a permanent reduction of lanes have a blue background; the arrows indicating the lanes are white. Signs marking temporary lane closures are yellow and the arrows marking the lanes are black.

**16** A cow (cattle on the road); a pony (wild horses or ponies); a deer (wild animals); a horse and rider (accompanied horses or ponies).

**17**  a.  No waiting for at least eight hours between 7 am and 7 pm on at least four days of the week.

  b.  No waiting for at least eight hours between 7 am and 7 pm on at least four days of the week plus additional periods outside these hours. The additional times will be indicated on plates nearby.

**18**  The stop line at traffic signals is narrower.

**19**  There is some form of hazard ahead and you should only cross the line if you can see that the road is clear well ahead.

**20**  A square of lights with trimmed off corners, with a diagonal strip of lights through the middle.

**21**  A ring road on a primary route.

**22**  The white sign with a black R indicates a ring road on a non-primary route.

**23**  They enable drivers to position their vehicles in the right lanes, ready to move off when the lights change.

**24**  You can cross the line if you are turning into a side road, if a traffic warden or policeman instructs you to do so, or if you have to avoid a stationary obstruction.

**25**  No pedestrians.

**26**  A level crossing and the junction of two important roads.

**27**  An oxidizing substance.

**28**  No loading or unloading during working days and at additional times, which will be shown on a nearby plate: for instance, the plate may say 'No loading at any time.'

**29**  A no right or left turn sign on the approach road, a 'no entry' sign or a 'one way street' sign near the opening to the road.

**30**  Traffic lights not functioning.

**31** A broken white line marking out a triangular space with BUS STOP written inside it.

**32** It means that you may cross the line so long as it is safe to do so and you can get back to your own side of the road before a solid white line begins.

**33** You should be prepared for low flying aircraft or sudden noise from aircraft.

**34** The entrance to a side road.

**35** A large white, square sign with a white P in a blue square on the left-hand side and the words 'Permit holder only' on the right.

**36** A tourist attraction or place of interest.

**37** The sign denotes a pedestrian route only.

**38** Look for a yellow sign with the letters HR.

**39** Low ground clearance, so special care is needed.

**40**
   a.   FALSE. The sign means that you should give way to traffic already using the major road.
   b.   FALSE. The sign means that you should change to the opposite carriageway.
   c.   TRUE.
   d.   TRUE.
   e.   FALSE. The sign warns of an unusual hazard ahead.
   f.   TRUE.
   g.   FALSE. The sign means No U Turn.
   h.   TRUE.
   i.   FALSE. The sign means that 30 mph is the minimum speed.
   j.   FALSE. The sign means that traffic merges from the left with equal priority.
   k.   TRUE.
   l.   FALSE. It is a hazard warning line, telling you that you should only overtake when you are certain that it is safe to do so and that the road is clear well ahead.

**41**  a.  No cycling.
      b.  Cycles only.
      c.  Cycle route ahead.

**42**  b.

**43**  b.

**44**  c.

**45**  a.

**46**  c.

**47**  A red-bordered triangle with a picture of a black zigzag of electricity and a plate underneath indicating the maximum height of vehicles which can pass safely.

# Driving Conditions and Hazards

**1**   You need to remember that it will take you longer to pull up than the smaller vehicle ahead.

**2**   To see and be seen.

**3**   Check your lights and reflectors and clean them if necessary. Also clean your windscreen and windows if necessary.

**4**   You may fail to see the direction signs. Move into the left hand lane early and keep a sharp lookout for the exit.

**5**   Check that your headlights are working and are properly adjusted and that your side and rear lights are working.

**6**   You should double it, at least.

**7**   It is about to bend sharply to the left.

**8**   The lorry is carrying toxic substances and is therefore dangerous.

**9**   Two pairs of alternating flashing red lights.

**10**   It is harder to judge speed and distance at dusk than when the visibility is good.

**11**   Long vehicles may have to take a different route from cars as they approach and negotiate the roundabout. You will need to allow them room.

**12**   Slow down and stop if necessary.

**13**   It is better to push your car off the highway. If you try to push it along the road you may obscure the rear lights and cause an accident.

**14**   Steady amber lights and bells warn of danger. Then red lights flash when the barrier is about to come down.

**15**  If there is one railway line, there is one diagonal cross. If there are two lines or more, the bottom half of the cross is reproduced underneath.

**16**  A sign warning of a roundabout.

**17**  You might interfere with emergency services if you parked your car at
   a.   A hospital entrance.
   b.   A doctor's entrance.
   c.   A police or fire station entrance.
   d.   A fire hydrant.
   e.   A coastguard station entrance.

**18**  Before overtaking, always make sure that the lane you are joining is clear far enough behind. Signal clearly and in good time.

**19**  You should wait until the vehicle in front is well clear of the crossing before driving onto the crossing yourself. If you drive across nose to tail and the vehicle in front stalls, you could find yourself stranded on the crossing as a train approaches.

**20**  Slow down, give them plenty of room and be prepared to stop if necessary.

**21**  Do not frighten them by using your horn or revving your engine.

**22**  You must leave enough room to allow for the possibility of a door opening or a vehicle pulling out or pedestrians stepping out from behind parked vehicles. At least 1 metre (3 ft) is essential.

**23**  Drive carefully and remember that children are quite likely to run into the road.

**24**  You should watch out for any vehicles that might be in the bus lane – particularly cycles.

**25**  Bear in mind that fog is often patchy and that, though the road is clear at the moment, you could suddenly find yourself back in dense fog again.

**26** FALSE. This only gives a false sense of security.

**27** TRUE. You may dazzle the driver in front and cause an accident.

**28** FALSE. You are probably going faster than you think and it is important to keep your speed down in fog. If you speed up you will reduce your safety distance from the car in front.

**29** FALSE. Another vehicle might be approaching.

**30** It must be treated as one crossing and you must wait for pedestrians crossing from the further side of the island.

**31** TRUE.

**32** TRUE.

**33** FALSE. Tinted glasses restrict your vision at night and could be dangerous.

**34** FALSE. You may only use the bus lane outside its period of operation.

**35** a. If there are pedestrians on the crossing you should give way. Otherwise you may drive on.

**36** b.

**37** c. You must judge the conditions and act accordingly.

**38** a. The Code reminds you that pavements are for people, not for vehicles.

**39** b.

**40** a. and b. You should never use hazard lights on a moving vehicle or use them as an excuse for parking in a forbidden area.

**41**  b.

**42**  c.

**43**  a. Driver travelling uphill have priority.

**44**  b.

**45**  b.

# Junctions and Roundabouts

**1**   Box junctions have criss-cross yellow lines painted on the road to prevent traffic jams building up at busy junctions.

**2**   Five: the four exits on the direction signs and the road on which you are approaching the roundabout.

**3**   A green sign with a yellow border and a large letter R in white.

**4**   You should slow down and make sure that your way is clear before you drive on. Be ready to stop if necessary and keep a careful lookout for drivers who assume that they have right of way.

**5**   Your position on the road and your speed.

**6**   They may need the whole width of the road to make their turn so you should give them room.

**7**   You exit on a slip road to the left; there are no right turns leading off motorways.

**8**   The centre or the right-hand lane, unless the signs or road markings give you other instructions.

**9**   The object is to prevent hold-ups and keep traffic moving at a steady pace.

**10**   A red-triangle with a broken circle of black arrows on a white background.

**11**   A min-roundabout consists of a painted circle or a raised circle at junctions on busy minor roads.

**12**   b. The car in diagram a. is too close to the left and would probably either run over the verge or swing out too far in the main road. The car in diagram c. has taken up a hazardous position in pulling out across the Give Way Line and the car in diagram d. has taken up a position more suited to a car turning right.

13 On signs at the side of roads or on the road as painted lane markings.

14 It is a red octagon with the word STOP in white capital letters.

15 Only when there is a large enough gap in the traffic to let you carry out your planned manoeuvre.

16 Cyclists, motorcyclists and pedestrians.

17 Other vehicles may cross in front of you unexpectedly as they make for their exits.

18 The regulations for mini-roundabouts are the same as those for ordinary roundabouts.

19 Each marker indicates the distance to the roundabout and each bar on the marker indicates 91 metres (100 yards).

20 The triangle would give figures indicated the height limit (e.g. 14' 6") with a small black triangle beneath and a larger black triangle above.

21 As close to the left as the safety and length of your vehicle allow.

22 The clearest convenient lane suitable to the exit you wish to take, both as you approach and negotiate the roundabout, unless the signs and road markings give different instructions.

23 FALSE. You must stop at the STOP line.

24 FALSE, If the road is clear, you should keep moving.

25 TRUE.

**26** TRUE.

**27** TRUE.

**28** FALSE. You must obey signals given by a policeman.

**29** b.

**30** b.

**31** a.

**32** Both a. and c.

**33** Cars B and C are behaving correctly. Car A should not have entered the box until the exit straight ahead was clear; car D should not have entered the box unless the exit on the right hand road was clear. Car C is allowed to enter the box, even when the way is blocked by oncoming traffic, so long as the right hand road is clear.

**34** b.

**35** b.

# Parking and Waiting

**1** A white 'P' on a blue background.

**2** Only in a lay-by.

**3** A zone where parking is only permitted at meters on payment of a set charge.

**4** A No Parking sign (a circle with a red border and a red diagonal line on a blue background) with the words 'meter zone' written underneath.

**5** In conformity with local waiting restrictions or a bus lane order.

**6** Never park on the road at night if you can avoid it.

**7** Goods vehicles not exceeding 1525 kg (1.5 tons) unladen weight and invalid carriages.

**8** Your vehicle must be parked facing in the direction of the traffic flow, parallel to the kerb and at least 10 metres (33 ft) away from a junction, or in a recognised parking place.

**9** Side lights, tail lights and registration plate lights.

**10** Parking is not allowed on a Clearway. You may stop only in an emergency.

**11** Yellow.

**12** As close as possible to the kerb.

**13** In fog.

**14** Make sure that the door is not likely to hit anyone, either on the road or the footpath. Look out for cyclists and motorcyclists.

**15** The exception is when the verge or central reservation is the only place possible for loading or unloading and so long as the vehicle is not left unattended.

**16** It would make the road narrow and could cause inconvenience.

**17** a. At or near a school crossing patrol or the entrance to a school.
b. At or near a bus stop.
c. On or near a level crossing.
d. On a footpath, pavement or cycle track.
e. Where you would obscure a traffic sign.

**18** Get out on the side nearest the kerb.

**19** You must make sure the handbrake is on firmly.

**20** The car would display an orange badge on the windscreen.

**21** While you are waiting for pedestrians to cross and at no other time.

**22** A double yellow line.

**23** The entrances to coastguard stations.

**24** Keep a careful watch for pedestrians who might step into the road without looking after dismounting from the bus.

**25** FALSE. You should never park on the pavement.

**26** FALSE. You are not allowed to park in an underpass.

**27** FALSE. You are not allowed to park on any road marked with double white lines, even when one of them is broken.

**28** TRUE.

**29** FALSE. On ordinary roads you are not allowed to park on the right hand side at night but this is allowed in one way streets.

**30** FALSE. Parking in cycle lanes is not allowed.

**31** TRUE.

**32** a. You would obscure the view of other drivers.
  b. It would narrow the road.
  c. It would cause danger to other vehicles or pedestrians.
  d. It would hold up traffic or inconvenience others.

**33** a.

**34** a.

**35** b.

**36** b.

# The Law and You

**1**  The Vehicle (Excise) Act.

**2**  a.  Road fund licence.
    b.  Driving licence.
    c.  Valid test certificate (if your vehicle is old enough to need one).
    d.  Motor insurance certificate.

**3**  That it is valid for the type of vehicle you intend to drive.

**4**  You should sign it in ink.

**5**  Drivers and front seat passengers in most vehicles.

**6**  That you are insured to drive it, either under your own insurance policy or under the policy of the vehicle's owner.

**7**  The speed limit is a maximum; you should not drive at 70 mph if this is too fast for the current conditions. You are not allowed to drive at 70 mph if you are driving a vehicle subject to a lower speed limit.

**8**  Your windscreen must be clean and your wipers must be in working order.

**9**  None. It is an offence to pick up or put down a hitchhiker on any part of the motorway, including the slip roads.

**10**  You must not use your horn in a built up area between the hours of 23.30 and 07.00 (11.30 p.m. and 7 a.m.). You should normally only use your horn when your vehicle is moving, except in emergency.

**11**  a.  It reduces co-ordination.
    b.  It increases reaction time.
    c.  It impairs judgement of speed, distance and risk.
    d.  It gives a false sense of confidence.

**12**   You should check with your doctor whether or not it is safe for you to drive or whether the medication might affect your driving ability.

**13**   You must stop and give your name, address and the registration mark of the vehicle to anyone with reasonable grounds for wanting them. If you cannot do this at the time, you must report the accident to the police within 24 hours.

**14**   A school crossing patrol with a 'Stop – children crossing' sign.

**15**   Make sure that his or her cycle has efficient brakes.

**16**   That the load is secure, so that it cannot cause a hazard by shifting or falling off and that it is not of illegal width or length. The vehicle must not be overloaded.

**17**   They must be efficient; it is illegal to drive with a defective or unsuitable system.

**18**   The legal limit is 35 micrograms of alcohol to 100 millilitres of breath.

**19**   The penalties are loss of licence for a long period and possibly a heavy fine or imprisonment.

**20**   Yes. You must stop your engine before you leave your vehicle.

**21**   a.   The carriageway.
     b.   The hard shoulder (except in emergency).
     c.   The central reservation.
     d.   The slip roads.

**22**   Your vehicle should be fitted with the appropriate number of mirrors and they must be fitted so that you can see the traffic behind you.

**23**   Your tyres must have a tread depth of at least 1 mm.

**24**   The driver must ensure that children under 14 are suitably restrained when they are riding in the front of the vehicle.

**25** Only one passenger may be carried and that passenger must sit astride, on a securely fitted seat, with proper rests for the feet.

**26** In a specially marked motorcycle section or at a meter, where this is permitted.

**27** Yes. When overtaking, you must ensure that you can get back to your own side of the road before reaching a solid white line.

**28** On the carriageway or on the central reservation.

**29** FALSE. It is 70 mph.

**30** TRUE.

**31** FALSE. If you normally wear spectacles, then you would be expected to wear them for the eyesight section of the driving test.

**32** TRUE.

**33** FALSE. One third of all drivers killed in road accidents are over the legal limit.

**34** TRUE. The tax disc must be displayed.

**35** TRUE.

**36** TRUE.

**37** FALSE. The legal blood alcohol limit is 80 micrograms of alcohol to 100 millilitres of blood.

**38** c. The law says that any vehicle must display a tax disc when it is parked on a public road, whether it can be driven or not.

**39** Either a. or b. would be correct.

**40** c.

**41**  a., c. and d. You are not allowed to stop to load or unload but the other three situations are legitimate exceptions.

**42**  In the case of a., b. and d. you would be committing an offence. Fitting fog lamps to your car is not obligatory so, providing you were using your headlamps in case of fog, you would be in the clear.

**43**  b.

**44**  a., b. and e. Children under 14 must wear *either* an adult seat belt or an approved child restraint.

**45**  c. You are not allowed to use a telephone handset while your vehicle is moving.

**46**  b. Vehicles towing trailers are not allowed to use the right hand lane of a motorway with three or more lanes.

# Other Road Users

**1**   A pedestrian crossing controlled by lights.

**2**   A zebra crossing has no lights but is marked by black and white stripes, lighted beacons and often zigzag markings on the approaches.

**3**   You are not allowed to
  a.   Overtake the vehicle nearest the crossing, whether it is moving or stationary.
  b.   Park or wait.

**4**   Harassing pedestrians by using your horn or revving the engine.

**5**   You treat it as two separate crossings.

**6**   If your vehicle has already crossed the stop line or you are so close to it that you risk an accident if your stop suddenly.

**7**   On the side facing the oncoming traffic, keeping as close as possible to the side of the road.

**8**   a.   Two elderly people walking (crossing for the elderly or infirm).
  b.   An adult and child (pedestrians on the road).
  c.   A man walking (pedestrian crossing).
  d.   Two children running (school ahead).
  e.   A man digging (road works).

**9**   The law says that both motor-cyclist and passenger must wear a helmet of approved design, securely fastened, on every journey.

**10**   On roads without footpaths.

**11**   Extend your right arm out of the window and raise and lower it two or three times.

**12** You should reduce speed and give them as much room as possible. Take special care on left hand bends, where you might meet them without warning.

**13** a. The blind and deaf-blind.
b. The disabled.
c. Old people.
d. Children.

**14** They carry rectangular signs painted in red and yellow slanting stripes.

**15** Outside the period of operation marked on the signs governing the bus lane, all vehicles can use the lane.

**16** Stop.

**17** The sign shows the rear end of a car towing a caravan, in silhouette.

**18** Be ready to pull in and stop as soon as you see a suitable opportunity, so that other vehicles can pass.

**19** A white stick with two reflectorised red bands.

**20** a. Halt your horse well back but do not dismount.
b. Keep going.

**21** When you are signalling.

**22** A passenger is allowed only on a cycle which has been built or altered to carry one.

**23** On bends and the brows of hills.

**24** Pedestrians are forbidden to loiter on crossings.

**25** A black and white flame.

**26** More than 1.83 metres (6 ft).

**27**  The marker shows an inverted triangle with slanting red and white stripes.

**28**  A white light should be carried at the front, a red light to the rear.

**29**  The outside rank of a long column should carry extra lights and wear reflective clothing.

**30**  a.  Crowded shopping streets.
     b.  Near a stationary bus.
     c.  Near stationary milk floats, mobile shops or ice cream vans.
     d.  Near parked vehicles.

**31**  Sturdy boots, gloves, light or bright coloured clothing.

**32**  On motorways or slip roads.

**33**  FALSE. Some pavements have signs indicating that they are shared by pedestrians and cyclists. On pavements without this sign cyclists are not allowed.

**34**  TRUE.

**35**  FALSE. It is an offence when the lane is marked with a solid white line.

**36**  TRUE.

**37**  FALSE. Trailers over 3500 kilograms (3.5 tons) maximum gross weight are classified as heavy goods vehicles.

**38**  TRUE – providing you can do so safely.

**39**  FALSE. Fluorescent material is more conspicuous in daytime or dusk but is not useful in the dark.

**40**  FALSE. A horse must not be led, ridden or driven on the footpath.

**41**  TRUE.

**42**  a. It is only once pedestrians have stepped onto a crossing that a driver *must* give way.

**43**  b.

**44**  a. b. and e. are prohibited. Only motorcycles under 50 cc are prohibited.

**45**  c. The only time you should sound your horn is to warn other vehicles of your presence. You should only use it when you are moving and it should never be used to show your annoyance.

# Rules of the Road

**1**   You should always drive at a speed that allows you to stop well within the distance you can see to be clear.

**2**   The safest way is to stop on the left hand side of the road until there is a suitable gap in the traffic, then turn.

**3**   Open both gates, then check that the green light is still showing before you cross. Then close the gates behind you.

**4**   Hazard warning lights and red warning triangles  Traffic cones may also be used.

**5**   The two second time gap marking the minimum space that should be left between two moving vehicles on the highway. You can check this by watching the vehicle in front passing a bridge or a bollard, then counting off two seconds before your car passes the same landmark.

**6**   Yes; it is an offence to open your door so as to cause injury or danger to anyone.

**7**   Where the road narrows and where it would involve driving over an area marked with diagonal stripes.

**8**   You must be able to exercise proper control over your vehicle and keep a full view of the road and traffic ahead.

**9**   Approach carefully, signal your intentions in good time and drive on only when signalled to do so.

**10**   You should give way to pedestrians at pedestrian crossings, when you are turning right and left and pedestrians are crossing at the junction and when you are entering or leaving property bordering the road.

**11**   You should wait in the side road until you can get right across the dual carriageway in one movement.

**12** Short, widely spaced bars.

**13** Red, red and amber, amber.

**14** A level crossing not separated from the road by gates or barriers.

**15** You know by the street lighting; unless signs show otherwise, there is a 30 mph speed limit on all roads with street lights.

**16** The horses with riders should be closer to you; the riderless horses should be on their left.

**17** Cyclists should carry nothing that might affect their balance or become entangled with the wheels or the chain.

**18** The STOP sign is octagonal and the Give Way sign triangular.

**19** You are forbidden to park on verges, central reservations or footways.

**20** FALSE.

**21** TRUE.

**22** FALSE. You should obey the policeman's signals and if he waves you on, you can ignore the STOP line.

**23** TRUE.

**24** FALSE. Learner drivers are subject to the same speed limits as other motorists.

**25** FALSE. You must stop when the barriers begin to descend or the gates start to shut, whether there are lights showing or not.

**26** TRUE.

**27** a. No entry for vehicles weighing more than the weight indicated in tonnes (including load).

b. No entry for vehicles wider than the width indicated.

c. No entry for goods vehicles over the maximum gross weight indicated in tonnes.

d. No entry for vehicles longer than the length indicated.

28  a. A hard hat.

b. Light-coloured or reflective clothing so that you can be seen more easily.

29  b.

30  a.

31  b.

32  a. The overall stopping distance for cars travelling at 50 mph is 53 metres (175 ft).

33  a. A steep hill upwards; in this case 20 percent, or 1 in 5.

b. T Junction.

c. The road is about to narrow on the right.

d. Vehicles are allowed to pass on either side.

34  b.

35  b.

36  c.

37  b.

# Motorway Driving

**1** Motorcycles under 50 cc, agricultural vehicles, invalid carriages under 5 cwt and slow moving vehicles with wide loads, unless specially authorised.

**2** The sign shows a two-lane road with a bridge across it in white on a blue background, with the motorway number alongside.

**3** You should check the radiator and oil level and fill up with petrol (or at least make sure you have sufficient petrol to get to the next service station). You should see that your tyre pressures are adjusted for motorway driving, in accordance with the instructions in your handbook. Check that any items carried inside the car or on the roof are properly secured, so that they do not become a hazard during the journey.

**4** You will need to assess road conditions more quickly than usual. Make sure you maintain your concentration and use your mirrors constantly.

**5** Forbidden manoeuvres are
   a. Turning in the road.
   b. Reversing.
   c. Crossing over the central reservation.
   d. Driving against the traffic.

**6** These are the roads by which motorists enter or leave the motorway.

**7** This is an extra lane running alongside the left lane at the entrance to the motorway. While watching for a suitable gap in the approaching traffic, you use the acceleration lane to adjust your speed to that of the vehicles already on the motorway.

**8** 70 mph.

**9** Keep your window slightly open while driving to allow fresh air to circulate and stop frequently at service areas for short breaks.

**10** For as long as it takes you to get used to the speed of the traffic.

218

**11**   Vehicles drawing trailers, goods vehicles with operating weights of more than 7.5 tonnes and buses longer than 12 metres (40 ft).

**12**   Only in emergency.

**13**   You can stay in the middle lane if you are overtaking a line of slow moving vehicles. Once you have passed them, you should return to the left-hand lane.

**14**   The sign tells you that you can reach the M69 by taking the A46.

**15**   It is for overtaking only. You should always move back into the middle lane and then into the left-hand lane as soon as possible.

**16**   Green studs are used to separate the acceleration and deceleration lanes from the through carriageway.

**17**   Stopping is allowed:
    a.   In the event of a breakdown.
    b.   In an emergency – for instance when stopping might prevent an accident.
    c.   When the police signal you to halt.
    d.   When red stop signals are flashing.

**18**   Only when the traffic is moving in queues and the right-hand line moves more slowly than your line.

**19**   Only at service areas.

**20**   They may have sharp bends and you should slow down in order to negotiate them safely.

**21**   Make certain that there is enough room for you to join the overtaking lane; use your mirrors and remember that it is easy to underestimate the speed of approaching traffic. Signal before you move out. Return to the left-hand lane as soon as possible, but make sure that you are not cutting in on the vehicle you have overtaken.

**22** Be especially careful in bad weather – rain, mist or fog – when the light is poor or in the dark.

**23** This is the extra lane provided on the approach to a motorway exit, to allow drivers to slow down before joining the slip road.

**24** The first priority is to get the car off the carriageway and onto the hard shoulder, out of harm's way.

**25** From the arrows on marker posts at the back of the hard shoulder.

**26** Rear end collisions.

**27** Proceed no further in that lane. If the red light is flashing at the entrance to the slip road, do not enter.

**28** It is more difficult to gauge your speed when you have been travelling fast over a long distance and your speed will probably be higher than you realise.

**29** A picture of a two-lane road with a bridge across it, with a red line drawn through the picture.

**30** FALSE. Vehicles already on the motorway have right of way.

**31** TRUE.

**32** FALSE. Learner drivers are not allowed on motorways under any circumstances.

**33** TRUE.

**34** FALSE. It is an offence to set down a passenger on any part of the motorway, *including* the slip road.

**35** FALSE. It is up to you to judge from the circumstances whether your passengers will be safer remaining in the vehicle or leaving it.

**36** b. On ordinary roads you would retrieve your case as soon as possible; on motorways you should summon assistance.

**37** b. You should never exceed the speed limit.

**38** a. You should never reverse on a motorway.

**39** a. On a two-lane carriageway you should drive in the right-hand lane only when overtaking.

**40** b.

**41** a.

**42** c.

**43** Both a. and c. are correct. Most motorways have signals on the central reservations but some very busy roads have signs overhead, so that you must obey the sign over your lane.

# Lights and Signals

**1**   A second train is coming. You must wait where you are until the train has passed and the barrier has lifted.

**2**   When indicators are not used or when you want to reinforce the signal given by your indicators – for instance in heavy traffic.

**3**   Red stop lights would come on at the rear of the car.

**4**   At a zebra crossing, so that pedestrians and other drivers will know that you plan to slow down or stop.

**5**   Flashing amber.

**6**   You must give way to pedestrians who are already on the crossing; otherwise you may drive on.

**7**   Uniformed police officers, traffic wardens and school crossing patrols.

**8**   A picture of a set of traffic lights with a diagonal red line crossing them out.

**9**   a.   Level crossings.
      b.   Lifting bridges.
      c.   Air fields.
      d.   Fire stations.
      e.   Motorways.

**10**   These are the lights of emergency vehicles so you should slow down and be ready to stop or give way.

**11**   Brake lights.

**12**   That your headlamps are properly adjusted, so that you will not cause danger by dazzling other road users.

**13**   When you might dazzle drivers approaching on the other side of the road or those ahead of you on your own side.

**14** At traffic lights on the road you may proceed when a signal light shows. At an automatic 'open' level crossing, the lights go out when it is safe to proceed.

**15** The regular lights are automatically controlled; the lights at pelican crossings can be operated by pedestrians who can press the 'Stop' button.

**16** If the number plate on the car ahead is illuminated, the driver has switched on his side and rear lights. If it is not, then assume that he is braking and act accordingly.

**17** You might obscure the lights from other drivers and cause an obstruction.

**18**   a.   Red and amber.
       b.   Amber.
       c.   Green.

**19** It could mean that the driver intends to move in to the left or stop on the left.

**20**   a.   Your left arm should be fully extended to your left, with the palm of your hand forwards.
       b.   Your right arm should be fully extended to your left, with the palm of your hand forwards.

**21** They should be carrying lights showing white to the front and red to the rear.

**22** Do not assume that the signal is correct; wait to make sure before pulling out.

**23** FALSE. You should only use fog lamps when visibility is seriously reduced. They should not be used simply because it is dark or wet.

**24** FALSE. You should proceed.

**25** TRUE.

**26** FALSE. You should not move off when traffic is already waiting on the other side of the lights to proceed in the same direction as you, so that by moving off you would block the junction.

**27** FALSE. Red and amber means STOP but you should be ready to move off when the lights change to green.

**28** TRUE.

**29** FALSE. You should signal your intention to go straight ahead by holding up your left hand with the palm facing forwards.

**30** FALSE. You must not park within 10 metres (33 ft) of a road junction.

**31** TRUE.

**32** FALSE.

**33** FALSE. This is the arm signal used by motorists; a motor-cyclist will extend his left arm and hold it steady.

**34** b. Dipped headlights should be used on high speed roads, even when they are lighted.

**35** c. When the amber light shows you should stop at the stop line.

**36** c. You should never rely on unauthorised signals. The Code says that flashing headlights should only be used to let another motorist know that you are there.

**37** b.

**38** a.

**39** c.

**40** c.

**41**  a.  The driver is about to move out to the right or turn right.

      b.  The driver is about to move in to the left or turn left.

      c.  The driver is about to slow down or stop.

**42**  a.  Vehicles approaching from behind must stop.

      b.  Vehicles approaching from both front and behind must stop.

      c.  Vehicles approaching from the front must stop.

      d.  Vehicles approaching from the front may proceed.

      e.  Vehicles approaching from behind may proceed.

# Safety on the Road

**1**   The purpose of flashing headlights is to indicate the presence of another car; they should only be used to let other road users know that you are there.

**2**   Safety posts mark the edge of the carriageway on potentially dangerous stretches of road; for instance where there are ditches or soft verges.

**3**   Red.

**4**   White.

**5**   Roads where there is no street lighting, where the streetlamps are not alight, where the lights are more than 185 metres (606 ft) apart and high speed roads, including motorways.

**6**   The thinking distance is the distance your car will travel in the time it takes you to react to a possible emergency. The Code calculates this distance on the assumption that brakes and tyres are in good order and that road conditions are good.

**7**   The braking distance is the distance the car will travel once you have applied the brakes – on the same assumptions as above.

**8**   Wipers and demisters.

**9**   In the rear seat, wearing an approved safety restraint appropriate to the age and size of the child.

**10**   It is best to keep the dog in the car. If this is not possible, the dog must be restrained (preferably on a lead) so that it cannot run into the road and cause a further accident.

**11**   Keep as close as possible to the nearside of the road.

**12**   Tyres and demisters.

**13**   You must always put on the brakes and switch off the engine.

**14**   Observe all signs, signals and speed limits. Check your mirrors, get into the correct lane early and adjust your speed. Keep a safe distance from the vehicle in front.

**15**   You should not drive if you are feeling tired or unwell.

**16**   You can fit child safety locks on the doors and make sure that they are secured each time you carry a child in your car.

**17**   You should drive slowly, keeping a lookout for children on foot, getting on and off buses or cycling. Stop when signalled by a school crossing patrol.

**18**   Drive more slowly and allow more distance between your car and the car in front; it will take you longer to stop in wet conditions.

**19**   You should approach with great care and be prepared to stop. Signal to other drivers when you intend to slow down or stop.

**20**   At or near
    a.   A junction.
    b.   A bend.
    c.   The brow of a hill.
    d.   A hump-back bridge.

**21**   Cycles cannot be seen as easily as larger vehicles. You should always give clear arm signals, especially at roundabouts and junctions.

**22**   It is more difficult to judge distance and speed on these roads, especially at dusk, in the dark and in fog or mist.

**23**   Near a school entrance, indicating that you should not wait or park there.

**24**   Open the window, switch on the radio if you have one, then pull into the next service area for a rest. Do *not* stop on the hard shoulder.

**25**   Hanging onto someone else's tail-lights is misleading and gives you a false sense of confidence. If the tail-lights disappear in thickening fog, you might assume that it is safe to accelerate and run into the back of the leading car.

**26** When it is dark and there is no street lighting and when you do not risk dazzling approaching vehicles or vehicles travelling in front of you.

**27** The windscreens, windows, lights, indicators, reflectors and mirrors.

**28** The bridge may obscure your view of the road ahead and some larger vehicles may have to approach in the middle of the road.

**29** That they are well away from the carriageway, from the hard shoulder and from the central reservation.

**30** Dangerous liquids may be leaking out onto the highway; dangerous dust or vapours may be carried towards you by the wind.

**31** Drive clear of the crossing, then close both gates securely. Telephone the signalman again to let him know that you are clear of the crossing.

**32** Your tyres must be suitable for the vehicle, inflated according to the manufacturer's instructions, free from cuts and other defects and they must have a tread depth of at least 1 mm.

**33** The picture shows liquid dripping from test tubes onto a hand and a black bar and corroding them.

**34** TRUE.

**35** FALSE. Children should not be carried in the luggage space unless seats have been provided by the manufacturers.

**36** TRUE.

**37** FALSE. Under normal circumstances you should not sound your horn when your vehicle is stationary but you are allowed to use it if there is danger caused by a moving vehicle.

**38** TRUE.

**39** FALSE. It is unsafe to use an ordinary household cushion. A specially designed booster cushion should be used.

**40** TRUE. Your thinking distance would be 6 metres (20 ft), your braking distance would be 6 metres (20 ft).

**41** TRUE.

**42** a. 30 mph.
    b. 60 mph.
    c. 70 mph.

**43** b. 50 mph.

**44** c.

**45** a.

**46** b.

**47** b.

**48** b.

# Driving Techniques

**1**  In dusk, darkness and fog and on fast roads.

**2**  You should never overtake unless you are sure that it is safe to do so.

**3**  Move quickly past slower vehicles, leaving plenty of room, then move back to the left of the road as soon as possible, without cutting in.

**4**  Give a motorcyclist at least as much room as you would give a car.

**5**  Look in your mirror often, so that you always know what is going on behind you and to the side of you.

**6**  a.  Before signalling.
     b.  Before changing direction.
     c.  Before slowing down.
     d.  Before stopping.

**7**  Use your mirrors and glance around.

**8**  You were travelling at 30 mph.

**9**  Cornering too fast, braking too hard or accelerating too harshly.

**10**  You should use the countdown markers to get into the left hand lane in good time; reduce speed gradually, signal and use the deceleration lane to slow down before joining the exit road.

**11**  a.  On motorways.
      b.  Out of a side road into a main road.
      c.  For longer than necessary.

**12**  You must make sure that the road behind you is clear and that there are no children or pedestrians in the way.

**13** The section of the road that you cannot see from your position in the driving seat.

**14** Ask someone to guide you.

**15** First mirrors, then signal, then manoeuvre.

**16** The 'One Way' traffic sign is rectangular; the 'Ahead Only' sign is circular.

**17** Cyclists may find it hard to keep a straight course when the road surface is poor or when wind is blowing.

**18** Pedestrians crossing between vehicles.

**19** a. Do not drive onto the crossing until you are certain your exit is clear.
   b. Do not stop on the crossing or immediately beyond it.
   c. Do not drive nose to tail over the crossing.

**20** You should leave room for other vehicles to pass on the left, whenever possible; keep a lookout for cycles and motorcycles; do not cut the corner as you turn.

**21** On left hand bends.

**22** 'Move only when you can do so safely without making other road users change speed or direction.'

**23** You must remember to cancel your direction indicator signal.

**24** TRUE.

**25** TRUE.

**26** FALSE. You should never reverse into a main road.

**27** FALSE. You should never overtake when approaching a bend. Even if you can see the road ahead, the driver in front might overshoot or swing out.

**28** FALSE. The signal of the driver in front may be helpful in telling you that you should pull out slightly to gauge whether or not it is safe to overtake, but you should never rely on unauthorised signals.

**29** FALSE. You should always glance round before moving off.

**30** Car B has the right of way. You should give way to vehicles coming towards you before you pull out to pass stationary vehicles on your side of the road.

**31**  a.    You cannot see that the road is clear far enough ahead.
       b. and c.    You might come into conflict with other road users.

**32**  a.    No.
       b.    Yes.
       c.    Yes.
       d.    No.

**33**  c. You must keep your speed at a safe level; the speed of another motorist is not your responsibility.

**34**  a., b., c. and e.

**35**  a.

**36**  c. The driver has taken up a position just left of the centre of the road.

# Lanes and Lines

**1**   White arrows.

**2**   The left hand lane.

**3**   When you overtake, when you are turning right or when you are overtaking a stationary vehicle.

**4**   Their purpose is to guide motorists, to warn them of hazards or to give them instructions.

**5**   Yellow lines on the highway mark 'boxes' at busy junctions.

**6**   Unlike an ordinary road, in a one-way street vehicles may be passing you on both sides.

**7**   You should choose the correct lane for your exit.

**8**   You should get back into the left hand lane as soon as possible, without cutting in on other motorists.

**9**   You should stop opposite the passing place, so that the other driver can pull into it.

**10**   The right hand lane.

**11**   The left hand lane.

**12**   When the lane markings indicate otherwise.

**13**   They are telling you to 'Get in lane' and you should move into the correct lane in good time.

**14**   The bus lane may be a contra-flow lane, so that you find buses coming towards you.

**15**   You should avoid moving unnecessarily from lane to lane and you should never change lanes suddenly.

**16**   You would be guided by any road signs or by lane indication arrows on the road itself.

**17** FALSE. Some bus lanes operate for 24 hours, others for a shorter time, which will be indicated by plates nearby.

**18** FALSE. Cyclists may only use bus lanes when the sign indicates that they are shared.

**19** FALSE. You should not use the lanes on the right hand half of the road unless signs and markings tell you that this is allowed.

**20** FALSE. On a three lane carriageway the middle lane can be used for overtaking.

**21** TRUE.

**22** FALSE. You may cross a hazard warning line providing you can see that the road is clear well ahead of you.

**23**  a. White studs mark the lanes or the centre of the road.
  b. Red studs mark the edge of the carriageway on the left-hand side.
  c. Amber studs are used by the central reservation of dual carriageways.
  d. Green are used across side roads and lay-bys.

**24** Car B has taken the correct route, moving into the deceleration lane ready to slow down before moving into the slip road.

**25**  a.

**26**  a. Lane lines have short white markings and long gaps.
  b. Warning lines have long white markings and short gaps.
  c. Centre lines have white markings and equal length gaps.

**27** Neither; traffic coming from right and left have equal rights to use the centre lane for overtaking, so both must exercise caution.

**28**  b. Approaching traffic should give way to traffic already using the roundabout, unless road markings indicate otherwise.

**29**  c.

# Breakdowns and Accidents

**1**   To get your car off the road as soon as possible, so that it presents no danger to other vehicles.

**2**   Other vehicles may hit the driver or pedestrians, so everyone should keep as far off the road as possible.

**3**   Hazard warning lights; amber winkers that flash on and off to warn other drivers of breakdowns or accidents.

**4**   Vehicles stopping or moving very slowly, hazard warning lights, the flashing lights or emergency vehicles.

**5**   Slow down, stop, take steps to warn other road users.

**6**   Fire.

**7**   Switch off engines and make sure that no one smokes.

**8**   You should
   a.  Warn other road users.
   b.  Notify the emergency services.
   c.  Remove the casualties if they are in immediate danger.
   d.  Get all those who are not injured to a safe place away from traffic.
   e.  Stay at the scene of the accident until help arrives.

**9**   Drive to the next emergency phone or ask the next driver on the scene to drive around the obstruction to phone for help, while you help those involved.

**10**   The location of the accident, the number of vehicles involved, details of any casualties.

**11**   a., c., d., e. and f. Only the cat is not mentioned in the act.

**12**   It means that the lorry is carrying potentially dangerous goods.

**13**   You should note what the sign says (e.g. corrosive or flammable liquid) and include the information when you notify the emergency services. Keep everyone away from the vehicle. If it is necessary to act to safe life, you should exercise great caution. Beware of any leakage or dangerous vapours.

**14** Leave the car and get yourself and your passengers well clear of the crossing.

**15** Get everyone out of the car as above, then use the telephone at the crossing to notify the signalman. If you have time before there is any warning of an approaching train, move the car off the crossing, then phone the signalman again to tell him that the obstruction has been removed.

**16** Always carry a first aid kit and learn first aid.

**17** Apply firm hand pressure, using some clean material if possible. A pad can be tied securely with a length of material.

**18** Pressing any foreign body into the wound.

**19** Be reassuring; make sure that the casualty is warm and comfortable; see that he is not left alone and does not move about unnecessarily.

**20** You must
    a. Stop.
    b. Give your name and address and the registration mark of your vehicle to anyone with reasonable grounds for requiring them. If you are not the owner of the car, you should also give the owner's name and address.

**21** Report the accident to the police as soon as possible, at the latest within 24 hours.

**22** Neither. Casualties should be given nothing to drink.

**23** Make way.

**24** TRUE.

**25**  FALSE. The last cone should be level with the outside of the vehicle.

**26**  FALSE. Though you would summon assistance if this happened on a motorway, on an ordinary road you should retrieve the dinghy as soon as it is safe to do so.

**27**  FALSE. Your stopping distance at 40 mph is 36m (120 ft).

**28**  TRUE.

**29**  FALSE. You should repeat the action every four seconds.

**30**  b. You should never cross the carriageway of a motorway.

**31**  d. You may obscure the rear lights so that approaching motorists cannot see your vehicle.

**32**  c.

**33**  b. Raising the limb should lessen the bleeding.

**34**  b.

**35**  a. Moving an injured person may result in further injury so casualties should be left where they are until medical help arrives. You should only move them if they are in danger.

# Miscellaneous

**1** Speeds on motorways often seem slower than they actually are.

**2** Pelican crossings.

**3** Motorcycles and cycles are less easy to see than larger vehicles and, at the same time, more vulnerable.

**4** Your view of approaching traffic may be obscured by other vehicles, so keep a careful lookout.

**5** You must not carry so many passengers that it is likely to cause danger.

**6** Yes. It is an offence to drive a vehicle giving out excessive fumes and smoke.

**7** You should always leave the window slightly open if you leave children or pets in the car, so that they have enough air.

**8** In a well-lit area.

**9** a. Remove the ignition key and engage the steering lock.
    b. Lock the car, including the boot.
    c. Make sure that the windows are tightly shut.
    d. Take your possessions with you or lock them in the boot; leave nothing on display.

**10** As well as using your mirror, you should look around to make sure that it is safe to pull out.

**11** a. Look behind to make sure that nothing is coming.
    b. Give a clear arm signal.
    c. Look out for bumps in the road, pot-holes or anything that might cause you to swerve.

**12** As you have not been able to exchange details with the owner of the vehicle you have damaged, you must report the accident to the police as soon as possible and in any case within 24 hours.

**13** Level crossings with gates or full barriers.

**14** You should overtake on the right; do not move to the left to overtake; do not overtake on the hard shoulder.

**15** Failing to adjust to ordinary road conditions, in particular driving too fast.

**16** You must ensure that you can control the horse in traffic.

**17** A red-edged triangle showing a car whose wheels are throwing up loose chippings.

**18** It probably means that a herd of animals is approaching. Those herding animals are advised to send someone ahead to warn approaching drivers at dangerous places such as bends and the brows of hills.

**19** You might see blue flashing lamps, hear sirens, two tone horns or bells.

**20** Signals must always be given correctly, clearly and in good time.

**21** Invalid carriages under 5 cwt are not allowed on motorways.

**22** Children should not be carried in the luggage space of estate cars or a hatchback unless proper seats have been fitted.

**23** Yes. You must ensure that your lights are in working order and properly adjusted.

**24** You should always be able to stop within the distance you can see ahead; in the dark this means within the range of your headlights.

**25** a.   When driving large or slow vehicles.
     b.   When herding animals.
     c.   When the barrier stays down for more than three minutes without a train approaching.

**26**  You should apply the normal rules at each roundabout.

**27**  You need to watch carefully for 'Give Way' signs.

**28**  FALSE.

**29**  TRUE.

**30**  FALSE. The speed limit for a heavy goods vehicles on a dual carriageway is 50 mph; for cars towing caravans it is 60 mph.

**31**  TRUE.

**32**  TRUE.

**33**  FALSE. If your vehicle is on the road, it must display a current tax disc.

**34**  FALSE. Two out of three pedestrians killed or badly injured on the road are under 15 or over 60.

**35**  FALSE. Cyclists should ride in single file on narrow roads; otherwise they should not ride more than two abreast.

**36**  b.

**37**  c. You should drop back so that you are a safe distance from the car which has just overtaken you.

**38**  The sign may be a., c. or d.

**39**  b.

**40**  a.  9 metres (30 ft).
    b.  15 metres (50 ft).
    c.  21 metres (70 ft).

**41**  a.  14 metres (45 ft).
    b.  24 metres (80 ft).
    c.  55 metres (180 ft).